Best Of Manchester United

Sam Pilger

BEST XI MANCHESTER UNITED CREDITS

Publishing Information

Series editor: Paul Hansford

Cover design: Dane Gartrell

This paperback edition published in December 2012 by Calm Publishing Ltd. Printed In United Kingdom.

ISBN: 978-0957129122

The publisher and author have done their best to ensure the accuracy and currency of information in *Best XI Manchester United*; however the publisher accepts no responsibility for the information published herein.

For my son Louis, who shares my love of United

CONTENTS

THE TEAMSHEET

I WENT TO see Manchester United for the first time in March 1980 with my Dad at the age of six. They beat Crystal Palace 2-0 with goals from Mickey Thomas and Joe Jordan and I was hooked.

The history of the club soon lured me in just as much as the team of the day, possibly because in the '80s it was the only place where you could read about United winning the league title.

I recall reading about the great names of the past and then jotting down who would make it in to my greatest ever eleven on the back of an envelope, so I've been in training for this task for a while.

This would also prove useful for my first ever job as the staff writer, and then deputy editor, on *Manchester United magazine*, the official publication of the club.

This was in 1996, when the magazine was still the main source of club news. Even then there was no proper website and it was just before the rolling news of Sky Sports and MUTV (and a long time before the constant updates of Twitter and Facebook).

For a brief time, players were more accessible and less guarded. It was just them and us. We would approach them directly at the training ground, unhindered by press officers or entourages.

I got to know the players of the era, the manager,

and also interviewed a host of club legends, before moving on to be the deputy editor of *FourFourTwo*, and for the last decade, a freelance sports writer. No matter where I have worked, I have always written about United.

I have sat with George Best in a London pub and visited him back home in Belfast; sat with Sir Bobby Charlton at Old Trafford as he reminisced about the Busby Babes; written a diary of a season with Gary and Phil Neville; ghosted columns for Ryan Giggs and Jaap Stam; helped Ole Gunnar Solskjaer choose a suit; had a cup of tea at home with Bryan Robson and Mark Hughes; inadvertently had Roy Keane hauled into Sir Alex Ferguson's office; and probably best of all, had Norman Whiteside recreate his 1985 FA Cup Final winner with a salt and pepper pot and a bottle of ketchup.

In the autumn of 1996, I also interviewed a young David Beckham in a Manchester restaurant, when a television on the wall began to show the video for the song *Wannabe* by a new girl group called the Spice Girls. "Here, I do like that one in the black dress," he told me, to which I replied I actually preferred the ginger one.

This book lists what I believe to be United's greatest ever XI, having written about the club, and spent the last three decades watching them home and away, while adding my appreciation and insights from when I have interviewed and met the players.

The Manchester United Best XI is:

Peter Schmeichel

Denis Irwin

Roger Byrne

Duncan Edwards

Jaap Stam

Ryan Giggs

Roy Keane

Bobby Charlton

George Best

Denis Law

Eric Cantona

The decision to put Peter Schmeichel in goal was probably the most straightforward. United's two other European Cup winning goalkeepers Edwin van der Sar and Alex Stepney provided only fleeting competition. If I was choosing a greatest XI from the entire history of the game, Schmeichel would be in that too.

You would assume after 687 games Gary Neville would claim the right-back role, but though he always made the best of himself, he didn't offer enough of an attacking threat. He himself admits scoring just seven goals was a "crap total."

Instead I moved United's greatest ever full-back Denis Irwin across to right-back. Though he mostly played on the left, he was naturally two-footed and played his first season at United at right-back. A player of unrivalled consistency, he was brilliant at augmenting United's attacks, and could score free-kicks and penalties too.

At left-back is the captain of the Busby Babes Roger Byrne, whose life tragically ended in the plane crash in Munich two days before his 29th birthday, but by then he had already proved himself an exceptional full-back.

A place had to be found for his teammate Duncan Edwards. Blessed with both raw power and an elegant touch, his most regular position of half-back is now redundant but he was renowned for his versatility and also played in the centre of defence. Teammates and opponents all testify to him being the Busby Babes' best defender.

According to Sir Stanley Matthews, Edwards in defence was like "a rock in a raging sea", while Nobby Stiles recalled when United wanted to protect a lead during their dominance of the FA Youth Cup, they put Edwards in central defence.

While both Nemanja Vidic and Rio Ferdinand came close to partnering him, Jaap Stam was simply the best defender I have ever seen. Tough as teak and never outpaced, the Dutchman brought supreme authority to the back four as he was almost never beaten.

On raw talent alone, you could argue Cristiano Ronaldo is Manchester United's greatest ever player. The only United player to win each of the World, European and English Footballer of the Years awards, in six years at United he won every trophy possible, and yet I'm afraid he doesn't make the cut here.

The feeling always persisted Ronaldo was only ever passing through United, biding his time before Real Madrid called. As Oliver Kay once memorably wrote in *The Times* about Ronaldo's United career, "It was a rocky marriage, but the sex was great.".

It was important each player of this side enjoyed the best years of their career at United and Ronaldo is still young enough to reach greater heights in Spain. Crucially I wanted the side to capture the spirit of United and simply couldn't countenance including Ronaldo at the expense of either George Best or Ryan Giggs, both geniuses who always quicken the pulse with the ball at their feet.

In this side Giggs would play on the left side of midfield, and Best, brilliant with both feet, would start on the right with a licence to roam.

The decision to choose between Roy Keane and Bryan Robson in the centre of midfield was my hardest. In the '80s, Robson, along with Norman Whiteside, was my hero. He was a world-class player to be proud of during often bleak times but while Robson scored more goals, Keane edges it for bringing greater success to United with his presence and ability to inspire all those around him.

In 2004 I asked Robson: who the better player – him or Keane? "If you put 1,000 people in a room, 500 would say me, and 500 would say Roy", he answered. But history has been kinder to Keane and several members in that room will have swapped their votes by now.

In contrast, the selection of Keane's partner in central midfield, Sir Bobby Charlton – scorer of a record 249 United goals, a record 49 England goals and the owner of both World Cup and European Cup winners' medals – was one of my easiest decisions.

Up front Ruud van Nistelrooy and Wayne Rooney's sheer weight of goals, over 300 between them and increasing, made strong cases and Ronaldo could also be deployed as a striker. But ultimately it had to be a royal forward line, the two 'Kings', Eric Cantona and Denis Law.

They were meant to play together, too; Cantona, the "can opener" as Ferguson called him, would sit just behind Law, effortlessly penetrating defences to provide chances for the ultimate goal scorer.

I have set this side out in a traditional 4-4-2 formation but the players are good enough to swap and play in several positions, making for a more fluid 4-3-3 or 4-2-4.

Together these eleven players can boast a total of 4,697 games, 1,035 goals and 87 major honours for United, whilst earning 677 international caps.

My pace would certainly quicken walking along the Warwick Road to watch football's greatest ever goalkeeper, an impenetrable defence, and some of the game's greatest ever attacking talent playing together.

I. PETER SCHMEICHEL

Goalkeeper
The Crazed Viking

Honours 1991-1999 – 398 appearances (one goal); Premier League 1993, 1994, 1996, 1997, 1999; FA Cup 1994, 1996, 1999; Champions League 1999; League Cup 1992; European Super Cup 1991

In the team because he was arguably the greatest goalkeeper to have ever played the game

Quote "You get through on goal against him and it's a terrifying sight... Here is this big, blond Viking flying out at you" – Sir Alex Ferguson

Greatest moment The night he kept out Newcastle at St James Park to turn the Premier League title in United's favour in 1996

BEFORE EACH GAME during the '90s, as the Manchester United players filed out of the dressing room amid the clatter of boots on concrete, Sir Alex Ferguson would turn to his goalkeeper Peter Schmeichel and say, "Hey, big man, we need a clean sheet today."

Schmeichel would simply nod his head and in nearly half his games for United – an incredible 179 times in 398 games – he would deliver exactly what his manager had asked of him.

While the Dane's status as Manchester United's greatest ever goalkeeper is almost beyond debate, it doesn't quite do him justice. He deserves an even grander title.

"A better keeper never played the game," Sir Alex Ferguson has said, while a poll by Reuters in 2001 found he was considered to be the greatest goalkeeper in the history of football, ahead of legends Gordon Banks and Lev Yashin.

For his eight years at Old Trafford Schmeichel provided the basis for the most successful era in the club's history, giving his side an aura of invincibility and opponents a psychological barrier to overcome.

If a striker eluded Steve Bruce, Gary Pallister, or later on Jaap Stam, and found themselves one-on-one with him, they should have been favourite to score, but they still had to overcome their hardest challenge, for this wasn't any keeper.

Standing 6ft 4in tall and weighing 14 stone, broadly built inside his specially made XXXL goalkeeper shirt, Schmeichel appeared to blot out the goal. He would stay on his feet for as long as possible, heaping more pressure on a striker, and forcing them to make the first move.

"You get through on goal against him and it's a terrifying sight," said Sir Alex Ferguson. "You think, 'I don't fancy this. Let me out of here. I'm going to get murdered.' Here is this big, blond Viking flying out at you."

More often than not Schmeichel would win these duels, smothering the striker, tipping the ball around the post, making himself even bigger with his trademark star jumps he learned from watching hand ball, and getting anything of his body on the ball. He once had the imprint of a shot from Stan Collymore on the inside of his thigh for two months.

"I want my opponents to feel intimidated by my presence" he once said. 'Everything I do is aimed at undermining their self-confidence. Even a fraction of a second delay in shooting can make the difference."

Despite his hulking frame Schmeichel could also be remarkably agile, flying through the air to catch a ball and reaching shots that appeared destined for the back of the net.

He could stop the roars of opposition fans as they traveled up their throats, clawing back shots before they could cross the line.

Witness his save from John Barnes against Newcastle in 1997, voted the Premier League Save of the Decade, or the header he reached from Rapid Vienna's Rene Wagner in 1996, prompting the headline "The Greatest Save Ever?" and comparisons to the goalkeeping gold standard, Gordon Banks' save from Pele at the 1970 World Cup finals.

Schmeichel was more than just a goalkeeper. Consumed with a crazed desire to win, he would demand the same from his teammates; snarling, shouting, cajoling and marshalling them from the back.

"He was one of those ferociously driven players who made all the young lads realise what it took to reach the top," Gary Neville once said. "He could be brutal, but that was just his raging desire to win."

"Peter craved perfection so much he would rant and rave if he had a shot to save but it was his way of keeping his concentration," recalled Steve Bruce, the victim of many of his tirades on the pitch.

"An aggressive loud mouth," is how Schmeichel once admitted to me he must appear to be on the pitch during an interview at United's training ground in 1997, as he sat in his sweaty training gear with a cut lip and a patchwork of bruises on both legs.

"It is my way of feeding my energy in to my concentration," he once said. "If you take the [shouting] away from me, I would be an ordinary goalkeeper. I've tried to restrain myself and it just doesn't work. I use my temper to stay alert, to stay focused, and to feel that I am constantly part of the game. It is essential for me to be at my best."

On the pitch, he had too much of this energy, too much talent, to stay confined to the penalty area. Ferguson once said: "He sees himself as an attacking goalkeeper," acting almost as a quarterback whose long throws to Ryan Giggs or Andrei Kanchelskis would begin attacks.

"Those throws are outstanding," Ferguson added. "Like Glenn Hoddle's passes, taking out half a dozen opponents in one go."

He was always willing to throw himself in to the opposition box at the death of games, becoming the first United keeper to score from open play with a header against Rotor Volgograd at Old Trafford in 1996.

"What the hell is he doing," was Ferguson's thought when he saw Schmeichel sprinting past him at the Nou Camp when United were a goal down to Bayern Munich in added time in the Champions League final. But the Dane's presence in the area unsettled the German defenders and helped secure an equaliser to begin that dramatic comeback.

Schmeichel never wanted to be loved, just respected by teammates and feared by opponents. He never courted popularity inside the dressing room. As a young player Gary Neville found Steve Bruce and Paul Ince helpful, but describes Schmeichel as a "different animal."

"I had to give him crossing practice and if I hit even one bad ball he'd shout, 'What's he training with us for? He's f***ing shite.'"

"Schmeichel was a poser," Roy Keane wrote in his autobiography. "He fancied himself in a big way and played to the crowd. It was all about him. All the finger pointing and gestures of frustration were designed to convey a message to the fans: look at me, how much longer can I go on performing miracles to save this team! This was an act mostly, but we didn't mind because his pose was what he had to do to gee himself up. To be fair, he was as good as anybody in the world... The fannying-around was a small price to pay."

Schmeichel could be a prickly interviewee, refusing to answer questions, while telling you other questions were ridiculous, but he was a deep thinker about the game. He never shied away from voicing his opinion, even if it was unpopular with the United fans, such as telling them he supported the hated Sky bid or that the vocal support at Old Trafford could be better.

Ferguson first came across Schmeichel in the late '80s when United were sharing the same hotel in Spain as the Danish side Brondby for a training break. "Instantly I knew I was seeing somebody very much out of the ordinary," the United manager recalled.

The United goalkeeping coach Alan Hodgkinson went

to Denmark on at least ten occasions to watch Schmeichel at a time when foreign players were still a novelty in the English First Division.

"My fear was he couldn't play here, but Alan said there was no doubt, he was a winner. He shouted and bawled at everybody, he was a real hungry bastard," said Ferguson. "I went to Denmark and I could feel it in his handshake. He thrust out this massive hand, and I thought, 'You'll do me'."

While a relative unknown in England, Schmeichel hadn't exactly been plucked from nowhere, and at 27 years old, he had already won three Danish titles with Brondby and was voted Danish Player of the Year in 1990. He once told a colleague of mine, "I wasn't a novice when I arrived here, I had already played 45 games for my country."

The son of a Polish pianist and a Danish musician, Schmeichel grew up as a childhood United fan whose hero was Gary Bailey. "I was bigger than everyone so players were frightened of me, I put pressure on myself and worked and trained like a mad man."

In his first five years at Old Trafford Ferguson had muddled through with Chris Turner, Gary Bailey, Gary Walsh, Jim Leighton, and Les Sealey but he knew to fulfill his aim of winning the league title he needed a commanding goalkeeper. He had to have Schmeichel.

After arriving for a fee of just £505,000, the Dane was quickly being hailed as the "Buy of the Century" by his manager. In his first season at Old Trafford he helped United win the League Cup and concede just 33 goals all season, as they narrowly missed out on winning the title.

Expecting to enjoy a break in the summer of 1992, Schmeichel was drafted in at short notice to play at Euro 92 with Denmark as a late replacement for the war-torn Yugoslavia, and helped his small nation create a minor miracle by winning the tournament.

It was Schmeichel's penalty save from Marco van Basten in the semi-final shoot-out that secured Denmark's place in the final where they overcame Germany 2-0 to become European champions. Schmeichel rates his fingertip save from Jurgen Klinsmann in the final as his best save, and the win, "the greatest day of my career."

Back at Old Trafford the following season, he played a crucial role in United becoming English champions for the first time in 26 years, and was voted the Premier League Goalkeeper of the Year.

The Premier League and FA Cup double followed in 1994, and after a rare barren year – despite Schmeichel conceding just two league goals at Old Trafford through the whole season – United once again won the Double in the 1995-96 season, with his heroic performance in a 1-0 win against league leaders Newcastle in March hailed as the turning point in United's season.

"People believe Eric Cantona won us the title in

1995-96, but Peter's contribution was just the same," declared Ferguson. "He was stopping goals, making great saves when the score was 0-0 or 1-0 to us. We had eight 1-0 wins that season which helped us win the title. He saves 10 to 12 points that other keepers are not getting their clubs."

Another title was added at the end of the 1996-97 season before Schmeichel announced he would be leaving Old Trafford at the end of the 1998-99 season, ultimately to join Sporting Lisbon in Portugal, citing a desire for a new challenge and to play under less pressure.

In his final season the Dane's experience and undiminished talent were essential in pushing United on to win the treble of the Champions League, the Premier League and the FA Cup.

It was on a turbulent night at Villa Park against Arsenal in the FA Cup semi-final replay that United started to believe making history might be possible. With the score 1-1, in the final minute Arsenal won a penalty and only Schmeichel could keep the Treble alive.

"I had lost my sense of time and thought there was about eight minutes left, so as Dennis Bergkamp placed the ball on the spot the full implications of the penalty hadn't really hit me. I was only thinking about saving the penalty. I gambled correctly and hit the jackpot."

United went on to win the game in extra time,

before securing the Premier League, and beating Newcastle in the FA Cup Final.

With Roy Keane suspended, Schmeichel was United's captain on the night they completed the Treble with that 2-1 win over Bayern Munich at the Nou Camp, and it was fitting he should bring to a close his eight years at Old Trafford by lifting the European Cup.

Schmeichel enjoyed two years in Lisbon, winning the Portuguese title, before being lured back to the Premier League for a season each with Aston Villa and Manchester City. He retired aged 39 in 2003.

Schmeichel, who now works as a pundit on Danish television, had once said when he finished playing he looked forward to sitting down and spreading all his medals and awards out on table in front of him to fully appreciate what he had achieved.

He'd need a big table. There would have been winners' medals for five Premier League titles, three FA Cups, a League Cup, a Champions League, four Danish titles, a Danish Cup, a Portuguese title, the 1992 European Championships, as well as a record 129 Danish caps, but probably his most cherished prize would not be a medal or a trophy, but something even harder to win: the title of football's greatest ever keeper.

II. DENIS IRWIN

Right full-back
The Cog

Honours 1990-2002, 529 appearances (33 goals); Premier League 1993, 1994, 1996, 1997, 1999, 2000, 2001; FA Cup 1994, 1996; Champions League 1999; League Cup 1992; Inter-Continental Cup 1999; European Cup Winners' Cup 1991; European Super Cup 1991

In the team because he almost never had a bad game. Incredible consistency whether he was defending or joining the attack

Quote "Denis Irwin was Sir Alex Ferguson's greatest ever signing" – Alan Hansen

Greatest moment Playing a one-two with Eric Cantona before striking it into the net against Tottenham in the 1992-93 season

ON THE EVENING of August 27, 2003, all four sides of Old Trafford rose to applaud the return of Denis Irwin, who was now wearing the gold and black of Wolverhampton Wanderers for what would prove to be his final appearance at the stadium.

A year earlier, after the season had finished, Irwin had quietly left United with a minimum fuss, returning to the club's Carrington training ground to pick up his boots and arrange for the kit man to forward on the rest of his remaining gear.

It seemed a shame Irwin, then the most decorated player in United's history, had to wait until this return as an opposition player to receive the loudest and most effusive reception he had ever received in a competitive game at Old Trafford.

The truth is the Irishman was taken for granted during his trophy-laden twelve years at Old Trafford.

Much of it was his fault for being so consistent. You rarely saw Denis Irwin have a bad game, or even a mediocre one; you came to expect sustained brilliance from him every week.

"I never have to worry about Denis," Sir Alex Ferguson once said. "He is a player who always gives you a nine out of ten game."

If you look at every celebratory picture of United players holding a trophy between 1991 and 2001, you will find Irwin in it, somewhere in the background, quietly satisfied with another job well done.

The Irishman spanned the generations from Ferguson's difficult early period when United were still searching for that elusive League title through the whole of the '90s when they dominated the Premier League and finally became European champions.

Irwin is the only United player to win both the European Cup Winners Cup in 1991, and the Champions League in 1999.

Despite this unprecedented success Irwin never sought adulation. "Full backs are probably just cogs," he said. "We will not win games, we are there just to keep the whole machine rolling on."

A friend of mine once said of any footballer he would most want to be Denis Irwin, because you got all the glory of playing for United, and none of the hassle. No abuse from away fans, no tabloids seeking scandal and no being pursued by paparazzi.

Genuinely two-footed, Irwin won most of his 56 caps for the Republic of Ireland at right-back, and played there in his first season at United before the arrival of Paul Parker saw him swap to left-back for the next eleven years.

He was the complete modern full back; quick, strong in the tackle and never rash, he possessed brilliant timing and an excellent disciplinary record. His reading of the game was superlative and he was always willing to make overlapping runs to send in his accurate crosses.

While deployed primarily to stop the opposition, Irwin was always a threat to them in their penalty area as well, scoring a total of 33 goals for United.

Witness the wonderful one-two with Eric Cantona, taking his lofted chip in his stride and scoring against Tottenham Hotspur at Old Trafford in 1993, his 20-yard winner against Coventry in 1993 to keep the title chase on track, or calmly finishing off a 27-pass move against Wimbledon at Selhurst Park in an FA Cup tie.

Before losing the role to David Beckham, he was also United's free-kick specialist, which included scoring against Crystal Palace in the 1995 FA Cup semi-final and against Liverpool at Anfield in 1994.

An admiring Peter Schmeichel once declared, "Denis was the best striker of a dead ball at the club because he could spin the ball, and bend it better than even Ryan Giggs."

"He was a really significant signing for us," Bryan Robson has said. "He had a bit of everything, he was terrific with either foot and could play on the left or right, he had pace, he could tackle, was cool under pressure, and he had a great attitude."

Growing up in Cork on the south coast of Ireland Irwin first honed his sporting talents as a Gaelic footballer and hurler, before concentrating on football after earning a trial with Leeds United.

Irwin travelled to Elland Road in 1982 and earned a

professional contract a year later, but after three years and 72 games, he was allowed to leave by manager Billy Bremner.

During the summer of 1986, a disheartened Irwin nearly returned to Ireland but was given refuge by Oldham Athletic in the old Second Division. "We could not believe we had got him on free transfer," Oldham's coach Willie Donachie recalled, but there was still work to be done.

"When he turned up, we were a very fit team, and this chubby-faced young lad got all red in the face and looked like he was about to explode before he got fit and went from strength to strength."

Irwin would play a total of 167 games for Oldham, two of the last of them were against United in the FA Cup semi-final and replay. His performances in those ties did enough to persuade Sir Alex Ferguson to spend £650,000 on bringing him to Old Trafford in the summer of 1990.

Irwin finished his first season with United winning the European Cup Winners' Cup Final against Barcelona in a wet Rotterdam, before becoming an important part of the first United side to win the title for 26 years in 1992-93. It was a campaign in which Ferguson valued Irwin's high standards, dropping him only once in 48 games.

In the 1993-94 season Irwin was United's only ever present in all 42 leagues games, and missed just one of United's 62 games in all competitions. United went on to win the Double of the Premier League and FA Cup and Irwin was voted in to that season's PFA Team of the Year.

In the summer of 1995, after a barren season, Ferguson decided to turn to youth, but while Gary Neville replaced Paul Parker, Nicky Butt was drafted in for Paul Ince, and David Beckham took Andrei Kanchelskis' place on the right wing, Denis Irwin, then approaching 30, refused to be ousted by this youth movement.

It was expected the emerging Phil Neville would eventually dislodge Irwin at left-back, but it never happened. The Irishman was just too good and too consistent to be toppled.

"I have always had to look over my shoulder," Irwin said while still playing. "Since the young lads came through it has given everyone at the club a boost, and it has made some of the older players keep going, which is what was needed... It makes us work harder."

This work would lead to Irwin winning the Double again in 1996, a total of five more Premier League title, and being the most experienced outfield member of the Treble winning side of 1999.

During the 2001-02 season, at the age of 36, Irwin finally relinquished his hold on the left-back position to Mikael Silvestre and left Old Trafford that summer for a new challenge with Wolves, the team he had supported as a boy in Ireland.

His experience helped to lift Wolves out of the Championship at the first attempt, allowing him to make that return to Old Trafford. And while Irwin's side beat United in the return at Molineux, they could not avoid being relegated. At the end of that season, after over two decades in England, Irwin retired at the age of 38.

He has remained in Manchester, and has settled in a career as a United ambassador and a television pundit for both MUTV and RTE.

As Irwin's career was coming to a close, Ireland's national broadcaster RTE commissioned a film about his life and career. It was an resolutely upbeat story of how he a boy from Cork managed to become Manchester United's most successful player, winning trophies, creating history and playing in the World Cup.

After filming in Manchester, Oldham, Leeds and Cork, and speaking to Irwin, and the men who helped shape his career – Sir Alex Ferguson, Roy Keane, Jack Charlton, Joe Royle and Mick McCarthy – the film makers showed the results to an RTE executive, who appeared unimpressed and simply said, "I think you need to get him to talk about David Beckham a bit [more]."

Not that he would have been bothered at the slight; he was always more happy to play the role as the shy and retiring character, happy to let others stand at the front while he got on with being a "cog."

But Irwin's role in United's success in the Nineties, and his status as one of English football's greatest full-backs should not be dismissed.

When Sir Alex Ferguson, Sir Bobby Charlton, Gary Neville, and Peter Schmeichel all chose their own all-time United sides, Irwin was in every one of them, while outside of Old Trafford, Irwin also earned a place in the Premier League's Team of the Decade.

When the RTE filmmakers interviewed Sir Alex Ferguson, he happily gave a glowing account of Irwin, who he considered to be the "bedrock" of several of his trophy-winning sides.

When they had finished filming, Ferguson enquired what exactly this was for, and was told it was a documentary on Irwin's career.

"It's about bloody time you did one," he told them.

III. ROGER BYRNE

Left full-back
The Leader of the Babes

Honours 1951-1958 – 280 appearances (20 goals); First Division Championship 1952, 1956, 1957

In the team because as the captain of the Busby Babes, he inspired all those around him with his stern authority, and pace and guile on the left side of defence

Quote "He was sure and smooth in his play, he carried the natural arrogance of a great player" – Nobby Stiles

Greatest moment In his first full season as captain leading United to the League Championship by a record margin of points

ON NOVEMBER 24, 1951, a 22-year-old Roger Byrne helped give birth to a new era when he made his first team debut for Manchester United alongside fellow youngster, 18-year-old Jackie Blanchflower, in a goalless draw against Liverpool at Anfield.

The day after the pair's debuts, the *Manchester Evening News*, seeking a way to celebrate the arrival of two such talented young players, christened them the 'Busby Babes'. A legend was born.

"It is hard to imagine a young player could make a more mature start," declared Sir Matt Busby after that first game. "[Roger Byrne] will play for England and when he gets in the team it will be impossible to get him out."

The United manager was eerily prescient and by the time of the Munich crash seven years later Byrne had won three League Championships, two as captain, and become one of the finest full-backs the English game has ever seen. After making his England debut he would play in 33 consecutive internationals until his death.

The original Busby Babe, Byrne was the leader of an extraordinarily gifted side that came to define an era. As their captain he helped lift United to great heights, as according to Sir Bobby Charlton "he had the true aura of a captain," who acted like a general leading a young army into battle.

As a player Byrne was also the leader of a new breed of full- back, who refused to simply sit back and defend, but instead would push forward to join in the attacks and make overlapping runs.

He read the game brilliantly and was never flustered; Charlton said he played with such calmness and described him as having a "personalised radar system," allowing him to anticipate danger.

He would often use his pace, rather than making a tackle, to retrieve the ball. "There was never a faster full-back," said Busby.

"I have never seen a better left-back in my life," said his teammate John Doherty. "Roger was very, very bright. He had brains and pace. Tackling was demeaning to him. He preferred to pinch it or make them give it to him."

"The art of playing full-back is to be able to make the winger go where you want him to," Byrne said. "It is fatal to rush into a tackle and you should bide your time, by backing away from the winger. You can place yourself between him and the goal, so that he can do the least harm...Tackling is a last resort."

Byrne played at the same time as two of football's finest ever wingers, Sir Stanley Matthews and Sir Tom Finney, but both always struggled to get the better of him. "I never saw either of them do anything against him. No greater tribute can a full-back have than this," said Busby.

Byrne was older and more experienced than the rest

of the Babes and some described him as aloof as he didn't socialise much with them. "I didn't have the nerve to speak to him freely because he seemed to be operating on another level of life to the rest of us," Charlton said, but he commanded absolute respect and as other Babes joined the first team he became their mentor and father figure.

"If you did well and scored a good goal, you would not expect more than a cursory pat on the back, yet from him it was a gesture you would prize very highly indeed," said Charlton.

He was different to most of his teammates. He was married at the time of Munich and while they would all travel by public transport, he owned a car, a cherished Morris Minor, which he once drove into the front garden of his manager's next-door neighbour.

And away from the club, while most played pool and went to dinner dances, he spent all his spare time training to be a physiotherapist at Salford Royal Hospital to have a profession in retirement.

Byrne was the conduit between the players and Busby. "He was the ideal link, because he was quick to help his teammates and to voice his opinions to Matt," said his teammate Bill Foulkes. "They could be heated exchanges but they had the perfect working relationship and great respect for each other."

On the night before the crash at Munich, as the players attended an official reception hosted by Red

Star Belgrade, Byrne could sense they were keen to celebrate their passage into the European Cup semi-finals elsewhere, and so took the lead, passing a note to Sir Matt Busby: 'You promised the boys they could leave once the formalities were over. Permission to go?'. Busby read it and nodded.

The players liked how Byrne would stand up to Busby and some fringe members of the squad once told Nobby Stiles, then a young apprentice, that their manager was "a little wary of Byrne, because unlike the others, he didn't lap up everything he said."

Born in Gorton, East Manchester, Byrne was a late starter, not signing for United as a professional until he was 20 years old.

Unlike Edwards and Charlton, he was no child prodigy, but instead left school to work as an apprentice in the laboratory of a dye firm, while playing for amateur side Ryder Brow. During two years of national service he was actually deemed not good enough for the RAF football side.

He was eventually discovered by the United scout Joe Armstrong playing in the Lancashire Amateur League and first joined United as an amateur before signing a professional contract in March 1949.

In the junior and reserves Byrne's attacking instinct often saw him as an outside left. He once scored a hat-trick in a 5-1 win against Bolton on the opening day of the 1950-51 Central League season.

An injury to Billy Redman saw Byrne make his first team debut as a left-back during the 1951-52 season but he would be used more as an outside left, helping United win their first League title in 41 years with a run of seven goals in the final six games of the season. *The Sunday Express* declared, "This kid is goal hungry."

At the start of the following season, Busby naturally continued to use Byrne in an attacking role but he didn't enjoy it, and so wanting to be used as a left-back, he rather rashly handed in a transfer request in October 1952.

Byrne spent two weeks on the transfer list, drawing interest from several clubs, but his stance would ultimately succeed when Busby took him off it and played him at left-back.

In April 1954 Byrne would make his England debut against Scotland in front of 134,000 fans at Hampden Park before becoming an ever-present in Walter Winterbottom's side at that year's World Cup finals. As Busby had predicted, once he was in the side he could not be shifted and played for 33 consecutive internationals.

In February 1955 Byrne succeeded Allenby Chilton as United's club captain and soon stamped his authority on the side. "He was morally one of the biggest men I ever met both as a captain and a person," Harry Gregg once declared. "He was a wonderful captain with real moral fibre to fight the club's battle with the players and the players' battle with the club. Roger was very much a man."

In his two full seasons as captain United were utterly dominant in the First Division and would win two League Championships, by 11 points in 1955-56 season and by eight points in the 1956-57 season.

Byrne was no showman, happy to let Duncan Edwards, Tommy Taylor and Dennis Viollet bask in the attention, but found himself voted *Football Monthly*'s Player of the Year for the 1956-57 season.

The magazine gave him this tribute: "Not only has he played in every England international but he led his side to victory in the League Championship for the second year, to the final of the FA Cup and to the semi-final of the European Cup."

"Though the fame of John Charles and Tom Finney have commanded a lot of attention, there can be no denying the wonderful stimulus given by Byrne to both England and United."

"His cool, calculated work at left-back, either when his men are in winning mood or fighting to avoid defeat, have been an inspiration he rarely plays a poor game."

Though he enjoyed success and an enviable life, Sir Bobby Charlton revealed in his autobiography that Byrne was troubled by what he called, "terrible superstition and some dark fears." His roommate John Doherty has recalled how he would wake up in the night complaining about terrible dreams and premonitions.

On February 1, 1958, Byrne captained the Busby Babes for the final time on British soil to a famous 5-4 win over Arsenal at Highbury, picking up a slight thigh strain, which at first was thought to have ruled him out of the trip to Yugoslavia for the second leg of the European Cup quarter-final against Red Star Belgrade.

However, Byrne recovered to make that fateful trip and led United to a 3-3 draw, which secured them a place in the semi-finals of the European Cup for a second successive season.

On the journey home United landed in Munich to refuel, but snow and ice on the runway held them up from continuing on to Manchester. After two aborted take-off attempts, the United party boarded for one last attempt, with Byrne noticing the tyre marks from the earlier attempts were now covered by the falling snow.

As the BEA Elizabethan aircraft hurtled down the runway for a final time, there was a sea of anxious faces inside the cabin, including Byrne, who gripped the armrests of his seat, and shouted over the roar of the engines, "We are all going to be killed."

Byrne died instantly in the crash. Harry Gregg has recalled how he found his body still strapped into his seat thirty yards from the smouldering wreckage. "He was dead but there wasn't a mark on him, he was always a handsome fellow, handsome in life and handsome in death," said Gregg.

Four days later, 21 coffins, including the body of Byrne, were flown back to Manchester. The roads on the 17-mile journey from the airport to Old Trafford were lined with mourners as the procession of coffins made their way to Old Trafford. Two days later, another large crowd of mourners would gather at St Michael's church in Flixton and Manchester Crematorium for Byrne's funeral.

Byrne left behind a widow, Joy, who he had married only the year before, and he never knew he was to become a father to a son, named Roger Junior, born eight months after the Munich crash.

Byrne died two days before his 29th birthday, and although he had already achieved so much, he still had much to look forward to. Sir Bobby Charlton told me had Byrne, and the rest of the Babes survived, England would have won a World Cup in either 1958 or 1962, while United would have become European Champions in 1958.

Beyond that, Sir Matt Busby's son Sandy believes his father was grooming Byrne to eventually succeed him as United manager.

The United goalkeeper Harry Gregg wrote this epitaph to Byrne for the foreword of his biography, "He was a man of integrity, warmth, intelligence and sincerity... A leader both on and off the field, he led by example, as his own high standards as a great captain bear out."

IV. DUNCAN EDWARDS

Centre-back

The Colossus

Honours 1951-1958 – 177 appearances (21 goals);
First Division Championship 1956, 1957

In the team because he possessed both unrivalled
power and grace. No one could get past him in
defence and no one could stop him when he strode
forward

Quote "He was the only player who ever made me
feel inferior" – Sir Bobby Charlton

Greatest moment Becoming England's youngest
player of the 20th century at the age of 18 years and
183 days

LESS THAN FOUR months before his life was tragically cut short, Duncan Edwards played one of his last internationals for England against Wales at Ninian Park in Cardiff.

On that day in November 1957, the Welsh manager was Edwards' mentor and Manchester United's assistant manager Jimmy Murphy.

Before the game Murphy stood in the centre of the Welsh dressing room, going through the strengths and weaknesses of each member of the England side in great detail.

He talked about ten players, but not Edwards, prompting Reg Davies, the Newcastle inside-forward, to put up his hand.

"What about Edwards?"

"Just keep out of his way son, there's nothing I could say that could ever help us."

Edwards inspired this kind of rare awe in all those who saw him play in the five years between his debut and his premature death.

The greatest Busby Babe of all, he has become an almost mythical figure, forever young. His legend is kept alive by only a few black and white newsreels and the memories of those who shared a pitch with him.

I once asked Sir Bobby Charlton to describe how good he was, and sitting in a box overlooking Old Trafford, he turned and looked at the pitch Edwards had once bestrode.

"He was the only player who made me feel inferior," he said.

"Duncan was without doubt the best player to ever come out of this place, and there's been some competition down the years. He was colossal and I wouldn't use that word to describe anyone else. He had such presence, he dominated every game all over the pitch."

"Had he lived, he would have been the best player in the world. He was sensational, and it is difficult to convey that. It is sad there isn't enough film to show today's youngsters just how good he was."

By the time he died at 21, Edwards had already played for United 177 times, winning two League Championships, three FA Youth Cups, an FA Cup runners-up medal and 18 England caps.

He had become both the youngest player to appear in the First Division at just 16 years and 184 years and the youngest England international of the 20th century, aged 18 years and 183 days, a record which stood for nearly 43 years before Michael Owen claimed it.

"When I used to hear Muhammad Ali proclaim to the world that he was the greatest, I used to smile," Murphy once said. "You see, the greatest of them all was an English footballer named Duncan Edwards. If I shut my eyes know I can see him. Those pants hitched up, the wild leaps of boyish enthusiasm as he came running out of the tunnel, the tremendous power of his tackle, always fair but fearsome, the immense power on the ball. The number of times he was robbed of the ball once he had it at his feet could be counted on one hand. He was a players' player. The greatest... there was only one and that was Duncan Edwards."

Edwards was revered for his all-round game and versatility, and how he could excel at almost every position on the pitch, whether it was centre-half, centre-forward, inside forward or half-back. "He was never bothered where he played," said Murphy.

However, he would make the majority of his appearances as a left-half, a hybrid between a defender and a midfielder, which was his favourite position as he was constantly involved and could use both his defensive and attacking abilities.

"He was Roy Keane and Bryan Robson combined, but in a bigger body," is how his former teammate Wilf McGuinness described him. "He could play as an attacker, creator or defender and be the best player on the pitch... He was world class when United had the ball, and when the opposition has the ball he was our best defender."

"Most players they are good at certain things; in the air, or good with their left or right foot, they read the game well, or they have pace. But Duncan had it all, he really was better at everything than anyone else," said Charlton.

"From the first moment I saw him he could play anywhere and do anything. He was brave, great in the tackle, could pass it long or short and score goals. When I arrived at United Duncan was the only player who could do things I knew I wasn't capable of."

Edwards measured 5ft 11in, so was by no means the tallest member of his United side, but his broad torso and thick legs gave him the biggest presence. The esteemed sports writer Frank Taylor called him, "A human dynamo built on gargantuan lines."

Former teammates and opponents all speak in hushed tones about his power and how players would merely bounce off him.

Edwards could muster a shot of extraordinary power. The Germans would call him 'Boom Boom' for the goal he scored against them for England in Berlin in 1956, while Jack Rowley, the scorer of 211 goals for United, said he wished he had Edwards' shot. Bobby Charlton distinctly remembers a goalkeeper once ducking a shot from Edwards and conceding a goal rather than trying to save it.

But Edwards' game was not simply based on his strength and size; he also possessed an impressive skill and flair. "Despite his massive muscular stature, he could bring off the most delicate of manoeuvres," said fellow Babe Bill Foulkes. "When he wanted to he was all flicks and swivels, almost like a conjuror."

Born in Dudley in the West Midlands in 1936, Edwards' prodigious talent first became apparent at secondary school. A Midlands scout called Jack O'Brien first brought him to Sir Matt Busby's attention in 1948 and United began monitoring his progress. However, his talent soon became so obvious they became just one of many clubs, including his local side Wolves, desperate to recruit him.

By 1952, panicked that they might lose him, Bert Whalley and Jimmy Murphy drove through the night and got Edwards out of bed in his pyjamas to sign the papers to join United.

In the early 1950s Busby had begun his grand project to produce a United side made up largely from home grown youngsters, which would in time become known as 'The Busby Babes'. Edwards would become Busby's greatest discovery, hailed by Murphy as "the diamond amongst our crown jewels."

"We used to look at players in training to see if we might have to get them to concentrate more on their kicking, perhaps, or their heading or ball control," Busby once recalled. "We looked at Duncan, right at the start, and gave up trying to spot flaws in his game."

Known by his contemporaries as 'Man boy' or 'Super boy' for his maturely developed body and game, his father once recalled how as a 10-year-old he could comfortably play with boys up to seven years older than him, Edwards first made an impact in the United youth side, winning the first three FA Youth Cups in 1953, 1954 and 1955 alongside his fellow Babes.

Before the second leg of an FA Youth Cup semi-final against Chelsea in the 1950s Jimmy Murphy had noticed his other players had become too dependent on Edwards, so he told them to take more responsibility. "Try to put more pressure on your own ability, there may be days when Dunc isn't around," he told them.

But United struggled in the first half, with Edwards not fully involved, and the rest of the side seemingly lost without their usual inspiration. At half time, Murphy changed tact. "Remember I told you not to automatically pass the ball to Duncan? Well, forget what I said. Give him the f***ing ball whenever you can."

It worked, and in the second half Edwards would score and help United reach another FA Youth Cup final.

Edwards was given the opportunity to transfer this ability to the first team when he was handed his debut against Cardiff City at the end of the 1952-53 season, before playing 24 times the following season and establishing himself as a United regular.

By the summer of 1955, Edwards was playing an increasingly crucial role for a United side that now boasted eight homegrown players. With an average age of just 22, he helped them win the League Championship by 11 points and so equal a record set by Preston North End in 1889.

United would retain the title in the 1956-57 season, accumulating 64 points – the highest in the league for 26 years – and narrowly miss winning the Double by losing to Aston Villa in the FA Cup Final.

After winning the first of his 18 England caps against Scotland at Wembley Stadium in April 1955, Edwards quickly proved to be a natural on the international stage as well, and prolific too, scoring a total of five goals from left-half.

The former England captain Jimmy Armfield said: "There is no doubt in my mind with Edwards, Byrne and Taylor we would have won the World Cup in 1958 and then four years later. England could have had a hat-trick of World Cup wins."

He captained England schoolboys, England Under-23s, and had he lived would surely have succeeded Billy Wright as captain of the senior side. It is difficult to play the 'What if?' game, but it has often been argued Edwards would have captained England during the 1960s, severely hampering the career of a certain Bobby Moore.

I once asked Bobby Charlton if Moore would have captained England's World Cup winning side at Wembley on that day in 1966, ahead of Edwards, who would then have been 29? "Probably not," he replied.

At the height of his all too brief career, Edwards was the best player in England but as Charlton said, "He wore his greatness lightly, but he knew it was a suit that fitted perfectly... His confidence never touched on arrogance, he was a lovely genuine lad."

He played in a very different era, when players would sign autographs on the pitch and travelled to and from the game with the fans on the bus, or even cycled. The only time Edwards was ever in trouble with the police was when he rode his cycle at night without a light.

Edwards was an endearing mix of confidence and courtesy. Before a game against Newcastle United, he strolled up to their legendary striker Jackie Milburn, and told him, "Reputations mean nothing to me and if you come near me I'll kick you over the stand."

Edwards kept his promise to a point – he didn't launch Milburn over the stands – but United won the game 5-2. "What a player that big lad Duncan was," said Milburn. "He was a nice lad too, for all his size and power and after the game he came back up to me and said, 'It was a pleasure playing against you'."

As League champions in 1956 and 1957 United became the first English side to play in the fledging European Cup, and in it Edwards thrived against the finest players on the continent, helping United reach the semi-finals in their first season before they lost to the eventual winners Real Madrid.

Edwards came third in the 1957 European Footballer of the Year poll behind the winner Alfredo di Stefano and Billy Wright.

In February 1958 United made it to the semi-finals of the European Cup for a second consecutive season with a 3-3 draw against Red Star Belgrade. After the game Red Star's Dragoslav Sekularac called Edwards: "Maybe the greatest player in the world."

On the way back from Belgrade, United's plane stopped to refuel in Munich. Amid the snow and ice, United's plane twice aborted it's take-off and the passengers returned to the terminal. Once inside, Edwards assumed they would stay overnight and sent a telegram to his landlady Mrs. Dorman in Stretford: 'All flights cancelled. Flying tomorrow. Duncan.'

But the captain of the BEA Elizabethan decided to make one final attempt to take-off, which ended in the crash that would kill 23 people, including seven of Edwards' teammates.

Edwards sustained terrible injuries, including damaged kidneys, broken ribs, a collapsed lung, a broken pelvis and several fractures of his right thigh, and for fifteen days he bravely clung to life.

In the days after the crash Jimmy Murphy visited Edwards in the Rechts der Isar Hospital in Munich accompanied by United's goalkeeper Harry Gregg, who survived the crash physically unscathed.

Gregg recalled how Duncan was lying still when they approached his bed, then suddenly opened his eyes and asked, "What time is the kick-off against Wolves? I mustn't miss that game." United's next game was indeed against Wolves that weekend. An emotional Murphy bent down to him and whispered, "Three o'clock son." Duncan replied: "Get stuck in!"

During those dark days, Bobby Charlton recalls visiting Edwards in his bed, and seeing how much pain he was in. A distressed Edwards asked where the gold watch Real Madrid had presented to him was, prompting Murphy to order a search of the wreckage. The battered watch was recovered and was strapped back onto Edwards' wrist, bringing him some relief and happiness.

But on February 21 at 2.15am Edwards finally succumbed to his injuries. He was dead at only 21. "I have seen death many, many times, but not like this," said one of the surgeons who tended to Edwards. "In all my years I have never seen a hospital staff so upset. This boy we have never seen before, he is so young, so strong... so brave. Ach, but he had no chance."

Maybe the passage of time has dulled the impact of this loss to English football, but imagine if Wayne Rooney or David Beckham had died at the same age. It is too dreadful to contemplate.

In the corridors of the youth academy at Manchester

United's training ground there is now an enormous 10ft poster of Duncan Edwards to inspire the generations that seek to follow him.

His memory lives on in his hometown of Dudley where since 1999 a large statue of him clad in an England kit has stood in the town's market place. There is an exhibition celebrating his life on permanent display at the Dudley Museum and Art Gallery and a stained glass window of him at Dudley's St Francis' church, while his grave in the town is still regularly visited by parties of United fans.

If Edwards had survived, it was believed his injuries were so serious he would almost certainly never have played football again.

The sports writer Frank Taylor, who survived the crash at Munich, and recovered in the same hospital as Edwards, wrote about his harrowing experience in his book *The Day A Team Died*.

"One of Duncan's nearest and dearest friends told me: 'Maybe it was better this way. The doctors said, had he lived, he might have had to spend the rest of his life in a wheelchair. Duncan couldn't have stood that. Now I can remember him as he was: the greatest thing that has happened in British football for years'.

V. JAAP STAM

Centre-back
The Big Dutchman

Honours 1998-2001 – 127 appearances (1 goal); Premier League 1999, 2000, 2001; FA Cup 1999; Champions League 1999

In the team because he was a Premier League champion every season at United, repelling forwards with his pace and strength

Quote "Without Jaap Stam, Sir Alex would still be Alex" – BBC Radio football correspondent Mike Ingham

Greatest moment Providing the defensive foundation on which United won the historic Treble in the 1998-99 season

EINDHOVEN MIGHT BE Holland's fifth largest city, but they still had to find the keys to unlock the airport when I arrived there with a photographer in the spring of 1998.

We had flown there to meet Jaap Stam just a week after he had joined Manchester United from PSV Eindhoven for £10.75 million, then the largest transfer fee ever paid for a defender.

It seemed an extraordinary amount, almost rash, to invest in a relatively unknown defender who had only won a handful of international caps and just three years earlier was still playing for Cambuur Leeuwarden in the Dutch Second Division.

"You are here to see Jaap, yah?" said our taxi driver when we asked to be taken to the PSV Eindhoven training ground. "Of course, 35 million gilders is crazy, but he is Holland's best player. Don't worry, he will be brilliant for United."

Set in an idyllic forest, De Herdgang is where PSV train each day in a relaxed atmosphere, reminiscent more of a pensioner's social club than an elite football club. A welcome change to the fortress-like English training grounds, the public are free to come and watch the players, and I see a group of men cycle in, lean their bikes by the pitch, and joke with Stam when soon after he nearly decapitates them with a miss-hit shot.

This was in the era before YouTube, Sky Sports News, and MUTV, so few United fans had actually seen any clips of Stam in action, let alone a full game, so I was curious to learn more.

Stam met me in the player's canteen, mingling easily with fans, and was clearly excited about joining United as I asked him what English football could expect from him the following season.

"Which other defenders would you compare yourself to? I've heard some even compare you to the legendary Franco Baresi?"

"No, I'm quite a bit quicker."

"How about Frank Rijkaard?"

"Yes, we are similar, but I'm faster."

"Are you a hard man?"

"A player recently came at me with a head-butt, so I grabbed him and put him in a head-lock... he looked a bit blue when I let him go."

"Arsenal have just won the Premier League title, how will you stop Dennis Bergkamp and Marc Overmars?"

"I have my ways... I can stop them."

"How did you deal with Ronaldo when you played against him?"

"He didn't give me any problems."

It soon became clear Stam wouldn't be lacking in confidence.

And over the course of the next three seasons, he would more than back it up, becoming recognised as the best defender in the Premier League, the best in the whole of Europe, and quickly earning a place in Sir Alex Ferguson's own all-time United XI.

In those three seasons, with Stam at the heart of their defence Manchester United were always Premier League champions, while he also helped turn them into European Champions for the first time in 31 years, as United won the Treble in his very first season.

When Stam had to hurriedly pack his bags after just three years, he left with winner's medals for three Premier League titles, a Champions League, an FA Cup and an Intercontinental Cup, as well as two UEFA Defender of the Year trophies from 1999 and 2000.

During this time, when Premier League managers were polled about which player they would most like to buy if given a blank cheque, it wasn't Thierry Henry, Michael Owen or David Beckham. It was Stam.

Veteran BBC football commentator Mike Ingham, said simply, "Without Jaap Stam, Sir Alex would still be Alex."

For those three success-drenched years, as Old Trafford resounded to the chants of 'Yip, Jaap Stam', he provided the foundation for all of United's cavalier and attacking football. They could flood forward knowing the big Dutchman, even without the security of a regular partner, had locked the back door and wouldn't let anyone in.

In the first leg of the Champions League quarter-final against Inter Milan in 1999 the Chilean striker Ivan Zamorano was stepping backwards when he bounced off the stationary Stam. He turned around, expecting to be given more space, but he bounced off him again as the Dutchman refused to give ground. The message was clear: 'You will not get past me'. He never did.

Stam was the complete defender; 6ft 3in tall and powerfully built, no one matched his strength, though he was very quick too. I never saw him lose a sprint to the ball. His instinctive reading of the game would help him get there first anyway.

"Once Jaap's pace took him into the channel ahead of an attacking player they had no chance," Ryan Giggs recalled. "He was so strong it was a mismatch. He would not be beaten."

At the final whistle he usually left the pitch with a clean pair of shorts for he rarely had to dive in with last-ditch tackles. He would simply use his pace to draw level with an opponent before whipping the ball away from their feet and giving it back to a teammate.

However, Stam wasn't all brawn; he could be incredibly graceful too, earning those Baresi comparisons. He was Dutch after all, so was always comfortable on the ball and could bring it out of defence with ease.

While his contemporaries Clarence Seedorf and Edgar Davids were at the Ajax Academy, Stam was a late developer, still playing at his local amateur side DOS Kampden before moving through a total of five clubs in six years. His talent soon came to the fore though, as he won a Dutch title and a Dutch Cup with PSV, as well as being voted the 1997 Dutch Player of the Year.

"The players didn't know much about Jaap when we signed him, but Jordi Cruyff said he was the best centre half he had ever seen," said Giggs. "We thought, 'Surely he can't be that good otherwise we would have heard of him.' But he was. From the moment he arrived he was brilliant. He was a beast of a man."

I once asked Peter Schmeichel, who played behind a succession of defenders during his two decades in the game, who was the best? "Jaap Stam," he replied. "He was a tower of strength. He was so quick and strong. In the Treble-winning season, he proved himself as one of the best ever defenders. He was awesome."

If he had a weakness, it was that he didn't use his size to score more goals from corners and free-kicks. Though he had a more than respectable return at his other clubs, he scored only once for United – and not even a header – a volley at the far post at Leicester.

During his three years at Old Trafford I was Jaap

Stam's voice. After that first meeting in Eindhoven I realised his honesty and directness could offer an interesting perspective on English football, and offered him a monthly column in *Manchester United magazine*.

A year later *The Daily Telegraph*, appreciating his frankness, also signed him up as a columnist, and I went with him as his ghost writer, producing fortnightly columns during the 1999-2000 season.

I also helped launch his website through *icons.com* during the dotcom boom at the turn of the millennium, and would speak to him about twice a week for updates.

As a result I got to know Stam well. He was always a pleasure to work with; a reliable, engaging and gentle character, he had no ego. He was a family man, who rarely ventured in to town, just a regular guy who to begin with had trained to be an electrician in a small Dutch village, but instead became the world's leading defender.

"Yeah, for sure, it's always nice..." became his endearing and amusing catchphrase, whether he was talking about winning another trophy, cutting an umbilical cord or on one occasion, hearing *Last Christmas* by Wham.

He was remarkably laid back. I once phoned him three days after Holland, the hosts of Euro 2000, had been knocked out of the tournament in the semi-finals by Italy when Stam had blazed a penalty high over the goal in the shoot-out. I thought he would be distraught, so I offered my sympathies. "For what?" he replied. The semi-final defeat. "Oh, that? No, it doesn't trouble me."

In the summer of 2001, Stam's candour would get him in trouble when his autobiography, *Head to Head*, ghosted by another writer, was published.

It detailed his journey from Holland to United and included stories about how Sir Alex Ferguson had allegedly tapped him up at PSV Eindhoven and was now encouraging his players to go down for penalties. He even went so far as to call the Neville brothers "busy c****", though Gary admitted they knew it was said with affection.

The News of the World had passed on serialising the book after reading it, but *The Daily Mirror* picked it up for a relatively cheap £15,000 and ran it for four uncomfortable days, featuring the headline 'SIR ALEX ACCUSED', and hyping up each snippet.

After featuring in the opening day 3-2 win over Fulham, Stam was dropped and not even given a place on the bench for the next game, a trip to Blackburn Rovers. It was assumed this was punishment for the revelations in his book.

But earlier that summer Ferguson has actually informed the United board he wished to sell Stam, believing that since returning from a four-month absence with an achilles injury he had lost pace and was no longer the same player. He initially wished to replace him with the French defender Lilian Thuram from Parma.

Stam always wanted to play out the rest of his career at Old Trafford. He had signed a new five-year contract earlier that year, and his wife had even ordered a new kitchen for their Cheshire house that week. So he was stunned to be called in to Ferguson's office and told he was no longer wanted. In fact, he was told, United had already accepted an offer from the Italian side Lazio.

Gary Neville can recall seeing a shell-shocked Stam stumbling out of Ferguson's office shaking his head, and saying, "I'm out of here. I'm flying to Rome to sign for Lazio tonight."

Neville told him he had to stay, while as the news spread to the rest of his mystified teammates most of them phoned him pleading with him not to leave, but he had no real choice – he had effectively been told to leave. Twenty fours later he was a Lazio player.

I spoke to Stam a couple of days later. "I didn't want to leave, but the manager said there was no longer a place for me," he said. He felt a mixture of shock, embarrassment, anger and sadness at leaving United. He didn't regret writing the book, only how it had been serialised, and Ferguson had never given him any sense he was unhappy with his form. He couldn't understand any of it.

"[It was] absolutely a footballing decision," Ferguson

explained, and he has never publicly said the book had anything to do with it. Asked if the Dutchman was not as effective after his injury, he said, "That's possible, you make decisions based on the evidence. I was not surprised by the uproar caused, Jaap was very popular."

The disbelief of United's players and fans was only exacerbated by Stam's replacement, the former French international Laurent Blanc, who at nearly 36 was on the wane and patently inferior to Stam.

Stam had always said he had no interest in playing in Italy but learned to enjoy it over the next five years, despite having to serve a four-month ban for testing positive for nandrolone, though he always denied ever knowingly taking an illegal substance.

After two years in Rome, Stam joined the reigning European champions AC Milan, for so long the home of Europe's greatest defenders, to take his place in an all-star cast alongside Cafu, Paolo Maldini and Alessandro Nesta. He played two seasons for the Rossoneri, including the 2005 Champions League final defeat to Liverpool.

Stam would return to Holland to play for Ajax for two years before retiring from football in 2007.

Ahead of his return to Old Trafford with Milan for a Champions League tie in early 2004, I spoke to him for *The Guardian*. " I don't hold grudges, Manchester United know they made a mistake in selling me. I haven't done too badly since I left, have I?"

This has since been acknowledged by Sir Alex Ferguson, who in a rare moment of repentance, admitted selling Stam in 2001 had been possibly his greatest "mistake" of his quarter century as manager at Old Trafford, a decision which had manifestly "backfired."

"At the time he had just come back from an achilles injury and we thought he had just lost a little bit. We got the offer from Lazio, £16.5m for a centre-back who was 29. It was an offer I couldn't refuse. But in playing terms it was a mistake."

The pair have since made their peace, and in the autumn of 2011, Stam, now a coach at Ajax, was happy to attend Ferguson's dinner to celebrate his 25 years as United's manager, for, as he has said, "Old Trafford will always hold the happiest memories for me."

VI. GEORGE BEST

Right midfield
El Beatle

Honours 1963-1974 – 470 appearances (179 goals); First Division Championship 1965, 1967; European Cup 1968

In the team because he was the most naturally gifted player to ever adorn Old Trafford. A genius that faded too quickly

Quote "It was paradise watching George play football" – Bobby Charlton

Greatest moment Scoring twice against Benfica in the Stadium of Light to inspire United to a 5-1 win in the second leg of the 1966 European Cup quarter-final

ONCE A MONTH at the end of the '90s I would venture to a modest, old-style pub on the banks of the river Thames in London to spend a couple of hours with George Best.

I was only a few years into my career, but was fortunate enough to have a private audience with arguably the greatest player the British Isles has ever produced to help him write his monthly column for *Manchester United magazine*.

The Phene Arms, just off the King's Road in Chelsea, was Best's haven for many years. He had a flat around the corner and came here to escape. The regulars all knew him and left him alone.

Best would always be on his own, settled in to a seat in the corner with a newspaper on the table in front of him and nursing a drink, usually a white wine spritzer crammed full of ice cubes.

He often looked frail, certainly older than his 53 years. Sometimes he would gently shake, and once he arrived with a bloodied face. But though he could never free himself from the grip alcoholism took on his life, there wasn't a sadness about him.

His eyes still twinkled with charm and mischief and he could be very funny too, delivering lines with a hearty chuckle that would make you genuinely laugh out loud.

Best was from the old school; an easy, lucid talker, he was warm and personable company. And though he was never shy in hailing his own talent – he was acutely aware of his value even today – he was seemingly bereft of any real arrogance.

Though he must have spoken about his career countless times before, he always relished doing it. He was never jaded by it, never rolled his eyes, because the memories of playing for Manchester United, when he was young and everything seemed possible, sustained him and continued to give him great happiness.

"The football pitch is sanctuary," Best once said. "It's a different world out there. Everything else is a million miles away. Nothing can replace that. It's a blessing at the time and a curse later on, because nothing can ever be the same."

When George Best graced the football pitches of England during the '60s and early '70s he provided weekly matinees of genius, evolving from a skinny teenage prospect in to arguably the greatest player Manchester United and British football has ever known.

He possessed every skill imaginable. He had incredible balance; he could simply skip past opponents, while his slight frame had an extraordinary strength that saw challenges, however brutal and late, bounce off him. His pace would leave all pursuers in his wake and his close control was unrivalled – the ball just stuck to his feet.

He was two-footed, playing most of his career on the

left wing, but he was far too good to stay marooned there. "Wherever the ball was, that was where I wanted to be," Best said. "The boss would tell me to do that."

"George Best was gifted with more individual ability than I have ever seen in any other player," declared Sir Matt Busby. "He had more ways of beating a player than I have ever seen. Every aspect of ball control was perfectly natural to him from the start. He could use either foot and his heading was devastating as well. He had more confidence than I have ever seen in any sportsman."

Years after Busby had ended his quarter of a century reign as manager at Old Trafford he was asked who was his greatest ever player? "Every manager goes though life looking for one great player, praying he'll find one, just one," he replied. "I was more lucky than most. I found two: Big Duncan [Edwards] and George. I suppose in their own ways, they both died, didn't they?"

Despite playing on the wing Best scored a remarkable 179 goals in 470 appearances for United and was the club's leading scoring in the First Division for five consecutive seasons between 1967-68 and 1971-72.

"The incredible thing is he didn't get the normal share of gift goals a specialist striker will get," marvelled Sir Alex Ferguson. "George Best nearly always had to beat a man to score a goal."

Best's artistry and skill is rightly celebrated, but he

was also remarkably brave, playing in the same era as Billy Bremner, Norman Hunter, and Ron "Chopper" Harris, who he famously evaded to score for United against Chelsea in front of the Stretford End.

"He has an utter disregard of physical danger," said Danny Blanchflower at the time. "He has ice in his veins, warmth in his heart and timing and balance in his feet."

"It was paradise watching George play," his teammate and captain Bobby Charlton once told me. "No one had seen his like before: someone who was so small and tough, who would go in to tackles, but also had the ability to turn people inside out and beat anyone he liked, he used to embarrass players time and time again."

"Yes, he could also be frustrating, he held on to the ball for too long, you would get yourself in to a great position and hope he would pass the ball, but most the time he didn't. However, he usually scored or made the keeper make a save."

Having never played at a World Cup finals – he called his 37 appearances for Northern Ireland "recreational football" – it is difficult to elevate him to same status as Pele and Diego Maradona.

However, the pair always wanted to make space for him. Pele once famously called Best, "the world's greatest player" and Maradona has often said the Irishman was his inspiration. England's World Cup-winning captain Bobby Moore said Best was a more difficult opponent than Pele.

"I have always been mentioned in the same breath as Cruyff, Pele and Maradona, and that's without having played in the World Cup," Best once told me when I asked him about his standing. "I have always thought I was the best ever player, that's the way you have to look at it. I have never looked at another player and felt inferior."

Manchester United were first alerted to Best's rare ability in 1961 when their Northern Ireland scout Bob Bishop sent Sir Matt Busby a telegram with the message: "I believe I have found you a genius."

In July that year Busby invited the 15 year-old Best to Old Trafford for a two-week trial during the summer holidays, and swiftly concurred with Bishop's judgement, giving his youth team coaches strict instructions: "Don't tinker with the boy's style. Let him develop his own way, naturally. He really is something special."

"I remember Wilf McGuinness, who was on the coaching staff, winding me up by saying, 'Bloody hell, if you think you're good you should see this lad from Belfast'," recalled Bobby Charlton.

On September 14, 1963, Busby handed Best his first team debut against West Bromwich Albion at Old Trafford. That afternoon he showed glimpses of what he could do; the Welsh left-back Graham Williams, who marked him that day told me, "I like to think I kept him quiet, but I could tell he was going to be one of the greats."

Best returned to the reserve team, before reappearing three months later to face Burnley. "I remember walking out of the tunnel and hearing the roar of 54,000 people," Best has said of the game in which he scored his first goal in a 5-1 win. "I was numbed, but at the same time exhilarated. There was no fear, not for a moment, and there never would be. I was born to do this."

For the next eight years, Best was at the epicentre of Manchester United as the third member of the side's 'Holy Trinity'. Comprising of himself, Denis Law and Bobby Charlton, their fluid and attacking football would conquer first England, and then Europe.

"I found it just as easy as it had been on the streets of the Cregagh estate," recalled Best. "The night before a game I would lie in bed and plot what I was going to do the next day. I used to imagine myself pushing the ball between the legs of the defender marking me; and the next day I would go out and do it."

It wasn't a mere coincidence that in Best's first full season in 1964-65 season, in which he scored 10 league goals, United won their first League Championship since the Munich Air Disaster.

The following season, still only 19, Best delivered probably his finest ever performance when he stepped into Benfica's Stadium of Light. The Portuguese giants had not lost for 19 European games, but Best proceeded to outshine the reigning European Footballer of the Year Eusebio with a devastating display, scoring twice in the first 12 minutes to inspire United to a 5-1 win and a place in the European Cup semi-finals.

"I don't know how he did some of the things. He'd go past people and you'd think, "How the...?' The little bugger run amok," recalled his teammate Paddy Crerand.

Best's life would never be the same again. On his return from Lisbon he featured on the front as well as the back of the newspapers. "That didn't happen to footballers in those days," he said. "The whole thing just snowballed after that."

Best was no longer a mere footballer; he was now glamorous, the game's first pop star, hailed as the fifth Beatle, or as the French legend and UEFA President Michel Platini once said, "the inventor of Rock and Roll football." This was the 1960s when Britain was casting off the bleak austerity of the post-war years and experiencing an explosion of youth culture, for which Best's dark good looks, sense of style and talent came to represent.

He became a fashion model, featuring in *Vogue*, and opened three boutiques in Manchester, while being used as the poster boy to sell anything from chewing gum to cologne, sausages and eggs.

"Life started to become crazy," said Best. "The girls wanted an autograph, and a lock of hair, and the men were almost as bad. I was having my first real taste of adulation and I would be a liar if I said I wasn't enjoying it. It had never happened to a footballer before. I was the first and it became a monster."

As early as 1966, he admitted, "Wednesday until Saturday is murder. I know I've got to stay off the town and get to bed by 11, but it drives me nuts. The only thing that keeps me sane is that there will be a party on Sunday and Monday and Tuesday."

Back at his day job Best helped United reclaim the League title in 1967, which was followed by his finest ever season. Although still only 21 years old, it would come to represent the peak of his entire career.

During the 1967-68 season, Best was almost unplayable. He was United's leading scorer with 32 goals, won the Footballer of the Year award and became the youngest ever European Footballer of the Year winner. To top it off, in the final game of that season, he helped inspire United to become the first English side to win the European Cup with a 4-1 victory over Benfica on a warm night at Wembley Stadium.

The truth is Best didn't have a great final. "I only played in snatches," he said, but this included scoring the goal that gave United their decisive lead in extra-time, with the now iconic picture of Best wheeling away to celebrate with his arm held aloft an enduring image.

"The skinny shy little boy who came off the ferry from Belfast seven years ago had done his job... if I hadn't been playing for Manchester United I don't think they would have won the European Cup."

This should have been the start of a long career, but it marked the beginning of the end, and Best would never win another trophy.

"From 1964 to 1969 he was the best player in the country," Denis Law has said. "However, it's sad as hell, but I don't think we saw the best of him. He went on the blink at a time when he could have got even better. You hit your peak at 28 and he was gone by then."

A year after winning at Wembley, after failing to defend the European Cup, Sir Matt Busby retired. And as the ageing Charlton and Law began to fade, Best was surrounded by inferior players he had little respect for.

"We'd beaten Real Madrid and Benfica, and now the Coventrys and Stokes were stuffing us at home, it was painful," he recalled. "What did I do? I went straight out and got pissed... When we lost badly, I went out to get absolutely slaughtered, to try to forget."

Best's last truly great performance for United came

in February 1970 when he scored six goals in an 8-2 win over Northampton Town in the FA Cup, and his last period of sustained brilliance was in the autumn of 1971 with 13 goals in 16 games.

He admitted his problems began in 1969 – "I gave up alcohol and women in 1969, it was the worst 20 minutes of my life" – and he probably became an alcoholic in 1972. It was in May of that year, on the day before his 26th birthday, that Best announced his retirement.

He returned to Old Trafford nineteen days later but in December, he walked out again. After ten months in exile, the new United manager Tommy Docherty invited him back for a final time. However in January 1974, after just twelve games in which a portly Best had struggled, he was dropped for an FA Cup tie at Old Trafford.

Docherty claimed Best had arrived at the ground drunk and with a woman, but Best always bitterly disputed this.

"After the game, I went up into the stand and sat there on my own," said Best. "I just sat and thought about all the good times I'd had... tears began streaming down my face. Eventually, a steward came up and said 'It's time to go, George,' so I got up and walked out of the ground." Best never played for United again.

After leaving Old Trafford, Best traded on his former glories as he passed through Fulham, Dunstable

Town, Stockport County and Hibernian, while he also crossed the Atlantic to play in the North American Soccer League for three sides. "It was a freak show, but I needed the money," he admitted.

He played his last game in England in 1983 for Bournemouth, before a brief cameo for the Brisbane Lions in Australia, but without the sanctuary of the football pitch, his life would steadily unravel as he battled with his alcoholism over the next two decades.

In 1984 he served three months in prison after being convicted of driving under the influence, assaulting a police officer and failing to answer bail. When he was healthy he could earn a good living as a football legend, but his life increasingly become tabloid fodder as he became involved in a succession of scrapes and scandals.

I last saw him in his native Belfast during the summer of 2001. He had moved to a remote house on the Northern Ireland coast with his second wife Alex to recuperate and escape the temptations of London and the Phene Arms.

Best had been seriously ill and he seemed frail and jaundiced. He shuffled rather than walked and his clothes hung off his weakened frame but he told me, "I have never been happier and I never thought that possible without football. My life is close to perfection."

Unfortunately it proved to be yet another false

dawn. Even a liver transplant the next year could not stop him drinking and he would endure a public and bitter divorce from Alex.

In November 2005, Best died aged 59 years old at a London hospital. While it was expected, it still came as a shock. After all, this was George Best – he always managed to pull through.

His former teammate Denis Law, who became very close friends with Best after they finished playing, visited him in hospital in his final days and sombrely stood on the pavement next to the Best family when the news of his death was announced. "Nothing could have been done to save George. It is difficult to tell someone to stop drinking. I know people tried," he once reflected to me.

On my final meeting with Best four years before he died, I asked him if he harboured any regrets? He shook his head with a cheery smile: "I wouldn't change a thing. I have had a great life."

VII. BOBBY CHARLTON

Central midfield

The Spirit of United

Honours 1956-1973 – 758 appearances (249 goals); First Division Championship 1957, 1965, 1967; FA Cup 1963; European Cup 1968

In the team because he was peerless as an attacking midfielder and came to represent the spirit of the club

Quote "He was as near to perfection as possible, both as a man and a player" – Sir Matt Busby

Greatest moment Lifting the European Cup in 1968 after scoring twice against Benfica in the final, ten years after so nearly losing his life at Munich

IN THE SPRING of 2005 Sir Bobby Charlton greets me in the lobby of the East Stand at Old Trafford, immaculately dressed in a blazer, slacks and a tie, before leading me up several flights of stairs to a hospitality box overlooking the vast green pitch.

Charlton couldn't resist going right up to the glass and staring down at the empty stadium, before turning to me with a large smile and saying, 'Isn't that a wonderful sight."

Though he has been ensconced at Manchester United for nearly 60 years, playing for the club 758 times and sitting in the stands for thousands more games as a fan and a club director since 1984, he still gets the same thrill at being inside Old Trafford.

He says sometimes he will just get in his car and find he has driven to the stadium, even when there isn't a game on, just to be there.

Charlton first set eyes on a very different Old Trafford as a 15 year-old schoolboy in the summer of 1953 after travelling by train from his native North East.

He was accompanied by an uninvited Sunderland scout, who had hoped to change Charlton's mind during the journey, but failed. There waiting for him on the platform was the United assistant manager Jimmy Murphy, who ferried him straight to Old Trafford.

Charlton can still recall being nervous and surprised

at how most of the buildings in Manchester were covered in thick black soot, but above all he was excited to begin his "big adventure". He didn't have any doubt he would enjoy a long and successful career at United and had even made plans for his retirement.

"My intention was to play for United until I was 35 and then become a greengrocer," Charlton told me. "My cousin Chuck was a greengrocer back in Ashington, and it cost him £2,000 to set himself up, so I thought if I played for 20 years and saved £100 a year, I would have enough to open my own shop."

Charlton kept to half of his plan; he played until he was 35 but when he finished at United, returning to the North East to become a greengrocer no longer had the same appeal.

Over those two decades, through both triumph and unbearable tragedy, Charlton had given himself to the club, nearly died for it and come to represent the very spirit of Manchester United.

"He was as near to perfection as possible, both as a man and a player," his United manager Sir Matt Busby once declared.

He became English football's greatest ever player; a champion of England and Europe with Manchester United – scoring 249 goals, a club record that still stands today – and a world champion with England, playing 106 times and scoring 49 goals, another record that still stands.

"He scored proper goals, not tap-ins like me," said Gary Lineker, who came within one goal of equalling his England record.

Charlton's brilliance on the pitch and modesty and quiet nobility off it would give him an unprecedented global fame. As Jimmy Hill once observed, he became "the most famous Englishman in the world."

While he was never cool like his contemporaries Pele and George Best, and even in his twenties looked older than his teammates with that infamous comb-over, he could match anyone's talent.

"I have more admiration for Charlton than any other player, even Pele," says his old German rival Franz Beckenbauer, while Pele himself called Charlton "a master footballer."

Charlton even sparked an unusual sense of jealousy in his teammate George Best. "I've never seen any player glide by defenders as easy as Bobby did," Best said. "I thought I was a bit tricky, going inside and out, but Bobby just strolled past them."

Nobby Stiles was the only player to win both the European Cup and World Cup with Charlton. When they played together, Stiles' instructions from both Sir Matt Busby and Sir Alf Ramsey were the same: Give the ball to Charlton. He considered it an honour.

"Bobby had something that separated him from

everyone else because he had this tremendous energy and grace," Stiles wrote in his autobiography *After The Ball*. "He was filled with natural power and wonderful balance, he could explode with either foot, and the first time you saw him play, you knew you would never forget that initial impact on your imagination."

"It was like seeing a great waterfall or a range of mountains for the first time. When you watched him play, you saw the beauty and the power of the game. It was a true revelation, and once you had it, you would always be a believer."

Charlton started out as an old fashioned inside-right, honing his attacking instincts before moving in to the centre of midfield, where he was stationed for his two greatest triumphs: the 1966 World Cup final and the 1968 European Cup final.

In the centre he could display his incisive passing, hitting it both long and short; but most of all, he could make straight for goal with his pace, ability to swerve past opponents and his equally strong left and right feet, before hitting one of his famously explosive long-range shots.

Charlton once told me his policy with shooting was simple: "Don't think about it, just hit the bloody thing."

"So many goals I scored were close to the keeper, but they were surprised by the shot so they didn't save them. Jimmy Murphy said, 'Don't worry if you miss, people will forgive you if you miss, but they won't if you have a chance to shoot and you don't'."

Born in 1937 into a large mining community in Ashington in Northumberland, Charlton was never likely to follow his father down the mines, for football was in his genes. His mother Cissie's four brothers had all played league football and her cousin was the Newcastle legend Jackie Milburn.

"I always found the game easy, and never had any difficulty controlling the ball, passing it or running with it," Charlton has said. "When I was growing up I used to play in our local park for about 10 hours a day. All the older lads wanted me on their side."

Soon there was more than twenty clubs asking him to join them. His family can recall instances when one scout was in the living room, while another waited in the kitchen, but Manchester United, tipped off by his school head master, were the first to come to Ashington.

"I had to peer through the mist," said the United scout Joe Armstrong of the first time he saw Charlton. "He was a gazelle and had the shot as hard as any grown man, but he was a kid of only 14."

Charlton made his debut at 18, scoring twice against Charlton Athletic at Old Trafford in October 1956 to earn a position amongst United's exciting young team known fondly as the Busby Babes.

"It was such a buzz because we had a really great

team, with players like Tommy Taylor, Billy Whelan, Eddie Colman and Roger Byrne," he says. "And then there was Duncan Edwards, who is without doubt the best player to ever come out of this place."

United retained the league title at the end of his first season to earn another foray in to the fledgling European Cup. "Matt Busby knew European football was the future," he said. "It was such an adventure for the players. We felt like pioneers."

"[That season] we were ready to become European champions. We were in the semi-finals against Real Madrid once again after getting past Red Star Belgrade. We were on our way home from Yugoslavia, we were in a great mood, I mean, the world was our oyster, and then the accident happened, and all our dreams..."

Sitting in that hospitality box, Charlton's voice suddenly trails off and he doesn't finish his sentence. Instead he is silent for a moment as he looks out across Old Trafford.

On February 6, 1958, the plane carrying Manchester United home from a victory over Red Star Belgrade in the European Cup quarter-final stopped to refuel at Munich. Amid snow and ice, and after two aborted take-offs the plane careered off the end of the runway, killing 23 people, including eight United players.

Charlton was thrown clear of the plane. The United goalkeeper Harry Gregg discovered him motionless, incredibly still strapped into his airline seat next to Dennis Violett, before dragging them both to safety.

Charlton regained consciousness and was taken to hospital where he was treated for shock and a minor head injury. The next morning a German in the next bed slowly read out the names of the dead players. "That was the worst moment of my life."

"Robert was never the same after Munich," his older brother Jack has said. "I saw a big change in our kid. He stopped smiling."

Charlton has said he thinks about the friends he lost in Munich every day, while the grief and guilt of their tragic deaths is something he has carried with him as a burden ever since.

"I would say football became more of a job than a pleasure. I still woke up on a Saturday morning with a rush of adrenaline, because I love the game, but things were different. Suddenly I wasn't one of the young players, I was one of the more experienced players."

"There was more pressure on me. I knew what we had lost with the young players at Munich we had to be put right. The European Cup almost became a holy grail. We had to win it for them."

Driven by such raw emotions, Charlton emerged as one of the world's best players during the '60s, teaming up with first Denis Law and then George Best, and winning the FA Cup in 1963, followed by

League Championships in 1965 and 1967.

In 1966 Charlton was voted both English and European Footballer of the Year, and topped it off by winning the World Cup with England. Scoring three times during the tournament, including both goals in the 2-1 semi-final win over Portugal, he was the Three Lions' driving force as they triumphed 4-2 over West Germany in the final at Wembley Stadium.

"That was the jam on the bread for me, but do you know what? It didn't completely satisfy me. I knew I would end my career with a sense of disappointment if I didn't win the European Cup."

Two years later Charlton honoured the memory of his fallen teammates by captaining United to the European Cup and scoring two goals in a 4-1 win in the final over Benfica at Wembley Stadium.

"At the final whistle, I felt more relief than joy," Charlton has said. "I was so very, very tired. It was an emotional night. We had won it for Matt Busby and all the boys who should have been there. The one thing I remember is how heavy the European Cup was when I lifted it – I nearly dropped it. But despite the tiredness, I think it was the best I had ever felt after a match, it was even better than the World Cup. For me personally, it was more important."

Charlton, who bowed out of international football after the 1970 World Cup, played on in a declining United side until leaving Old Trafford at the end of the 1972-73 season.

He decided he was unsuited to management after two unsuccessful years at Preston North End and retreated into more comfortable roles, running his Soccer Schools – which helped unearth David Beckham – and acting as the elder statesman of the game, campaigning for Olympic and World Cup bids. In the United boardroom, he has proved to be a useful ally to Sir Alex Ferguson.

Even now he still has the same sense of joy and wonderment at the unique role he has played in Manchester United's history. "I'm proud of what I've done... I know I really am a very lucky lad."

VIII. ROY KEANE

Central midfield
Robot, *Madman*, *Winner*

Honours 1993-2005 – 480 appearances (51 goals); Premier League 1994, 1996, 1997, 1999, 2000, 2001, 2003; FA Cup 1994, 1996, 1999, 2004; Champions League 1999; Inter-Continental Cup 1999

In the team because he was the most influential player of his generation, whose restless anger and presence in midfield galvanised all those around him

Quote "If I was putting Roy Keane out there to represent Manchester United on a one against one, we'd win the Derby, the National, the Boat Race and anything else. It's an incredible thing he's got" – Sir Alex Ferguson

Greatest moment Despite knowing he would miss the final, he still inspired United to a brilliant comeback win against Juventus at the Stadio delle Alpi in the Champions League semi-final of 1999

"NO ONE WILL remember me in 20 or 30 years time. In comparison to George Best, I won't be remembered. And that's fine – why should I be?"

It is the spring of 2001, and I'm sitting opposite Roy Keane in a photographer's studio in Manchester. At the time he is the best player in Britain and the reigning Footballer of the Year, so I am more than little surprised to find myself having to convince him of his standing in the game.

"Because you captained one of the greatest club sides of all time," I tell him.

"Ah, there's been a lot of great United captains: Steve Bruce, Bryan Robson, Eric Cantona…"

"But none of them enjoyed your success. You captained United to the treble."

"You tell me what that means? That was two years ago. That's the problem, people are always looking back. United won the European Cup in 1968 and didn't stop going on about it until we won it again."

"They would always talk about the great teams of the Ron Atkinson era who didn't win anything… OK, they won the FA Cup a couple of times. People need to set their standards a bit higher and not live in the past."

"Who ever said I want to be remembered anyway? Why should I worry about what people think about me in the future? I might be dead tomorrow."

It was this bluntness, lack of sentimentality and searing honesty that made Keane the most successful captain in United's history and has ensured, even if he doesn't care, that he will be always be remembered.

Manchester United's relentless success throughout most of the '90s and into the new millennium was based upon Keane's driven character.

Keane was Sir Alex Ferguson's voice on the pitch; together they shared an insatiable hunger to keep on winning. It is why Ferguson, after twenty years at Old Trafford declared, "Keane is the best I've ever had here."

"If I was putting Roy Keane out there to represent Manchester United on a one against one, we would win the Derby, the National, the Boat Race and anything else. It's an incredible thing he's got."

A complex and intense character, Keane was always simmering, always striving for perfection. He set the standards at United, even when they seemed impossibly high. He once acknowledged his image was that of "the robot, the madman, the winner."

This obsession with winning gripped him long before he arrived at United. "I could never accept losing. It's like at school, or at Rockmount [his schoolboy team]. The trainers would be going, "Relax, Roy," but no, that's not me. Mad, I know..."

The small details mattered to Keane. On his first day

of pre-season training with United in 1993 he ordered a taxi to drive to the Cliff training ground, and followed behind in his own car to guarantee he would not get lost. He also arrived an hour before anyone else.

In the following years when a new player like Mark Bosnich arrived late for their first day he made them aware he was disgusted they had not made the same effort as him.

On the pitch he appeared to be in a constant state of rage, Gary Neville has said he got exhausted just looking at him, and wondered how he didn't have a heart attack. Neville recalls being abused for taking one – yes one – extra touch of the ball before crossing it. "It was like having a snarling pit bull in your face."

"Keane's greatest gift was to create a standard of performance which demanded the very best," said Neville. "You would look at him busting a gut and feel that you'd be betraying him if you didn't give everything yourself."

"Aggression is what I do," Keane admitted. "I go to war...You don't contest football matches in a reasonable state of mind."

But revering Keane as a leader shouldn't obscure his quality as a player. He wasn't in the team simply to motivate others; he could play too. He might not have been pretty, with his scurrying running style, straight back and hunched shoulders but he had an incredible presence in the centre of midfield.

Keane did the simple work brilliantly. He was an expert at snuffing out attacks with his expertly timed tackles (he once admitted to me he would see players pull out of them against him), then wisely distributing the ball; he kept possession with ease, rarely wasting the ball and could often dictate the tempo of games on his own.

His stamina could not be matched and would take him up and down the field, surging forward to score at one end before tackling back at the other.

"I'm not capable of something magical, so my strength is my work-rate, and if I don't have that I may as well pack the game in," he once said. "I keep going when others maybe don't."

As a teenager Keane wrote to several clubs in England asking for a trial but not to Manchester United because he didn't think he would ever be good enough for them.

However, in 1990, at the age of 18, his performances for the Irish side Cobh Ramblers persuaded Brian Clough to sign him for Nottingham Forest for £47,000. He made an immediate impact in his first season establishing himself as a regular, winning his first cap for Ireland and collecting an FA Cup runners-up medal after losing in the final to Tottenham Hotspur.

The United scout Les Kershaw was at Anfield in

August 1990 to witness Keane's debut. He had gone to watch Liverpool, but was captivated by the young Irishman. "I have seen a player, a real player," he told his boss back at Old Trafford. Ferguson watched him once and declared, "We must have him."

But United would have to wait another three years, and pay a British record transfer fee of £3.75 million, before they could ward off a resurgent Blackburn Rovers and bring him to Old Trafford in the summer of 1993.

The Irishman turned a good team into a great one. United had won the Premier League the year before, but with the addition of the midfielder, they added the FA Cup to the title to complete the club's first Double. Keane was an integral part of a side many regard as United's best ever.

He soon became United's most important player, making light of Paul Ince's departure, to help lead United to another Premier League and FA Cup double in the 1995-96 season. In the FA Cup final against Liverpool Eric Cantona naturally drew the most praise for his dramatic late winner, but Ferguson declared Keane was the real man of the match for tirelessly smothering out any threat from Robbie Fowler and Steve McManaman.

Another Premier League title was added in the 1996-97 season, before Eric Cantona's retirement saw Keane, still only 25-years-old, handed the captaincy.

After only a month wearing the armband and

frustrated at United playing "crap" and losing 1-0 to Leeds, he flicked a leg at Alf Inge-Haaland, but caught his studs in the Elland Road turf and snapped his cruciate ligament. He would miss the rest of the season, and without him United relinquished the title to Arsenal.

Keane's year sitting on the sidelines turned in to one of both indulgence and enlightenment. Keane had always liked a drink, he even partly blamed it on picking up the injury at Leeds, admitting to getting in to a drunken fight with some fellow Irishmen at a hotel two days before the game. "My night of drinking had taken it's toll," he would write in his autobiography.

Since he had arrived at Forest the naturally shy Keane admitted he had drunk heavily, and had several scraps. It was all part of a night out. "That was the norm back then, we used to get wrecked," he has said.

At first, the lack of football only accelerated his drinking. "I was out on the piss every night," he said. "[It was] totally ridiculous. I was doing a lot of stuff I shouldn't have been doing, daft stuff like jumping over hedges and cars. I'd sometimes come in the next day and I couldn't move for my knee."

But as he went through his recovery he realised he had to change and cut out the drinking. "I'd watch the lads finish training, and they'd shoot off like the building was on fire, like they couldn't get away quick enough. I said to myself, 'If I do get back there, I'm going to work on the things I need to work on'."

In the summer of 1998, on the brink of his comeback, I spoke with Keane at the Cliff. He seemed like a man in a hurry, as though he wanted to make up for lost time. "I'm more hungry about the game now, being out helped me appreciate my position more." However, there was self-doubt too. "A day has not passed where I haven't thought 'Can I ever be the same player again?'"

He would prove he was the same player, probably even better, as in his first full season as captain he made the most appearances of any outfield player, was voted the club's Player of the Year, and above all led United to the treble of the Premier League, FA Cup and Champions League.

Throughout the Treble year Keane was the difference, and nowhere was this better displayed than in the defining game of his career against Juventus in the second leg of the Champions League semi-final at the Stadio Delle Alpi.

After drawing the first leg 1-1, United found themselves trailing 2-0 after only 11 minutes. It appeared as though United's hopes of wining the Champions League – and the Treble – were over. Luckily, no one told Keane.

Though he was faced with one of Europe's strongest ever midfields, comprising of World Cup winners

Zinedine Zidane and Didier Deschamps and Dutchman Edgar Davids, Keane chased a seemingly lost cause, even after being shown a yellow card which meant he would be banned from the final should United reach it.

"I didn't think I could have a higher opinion than I already had of the Irishman but he rose even further in my estimation," Sir Alex Ferguson wrote in his autobiography. "The minute he was booked and out of the final he redoubled his efforts to get the team there. It was the most emphatic display of selflessness I have seen on a football field. Pounding every blade of grass, competing as if he would rather die of exhaustion than lose, he inspired all around him. I felt it was an honour to be associated with such a player."

Gary Neville has admitted the players looked at the efforts of Keane, and realised they could win after all. Keane started the comeback himself, glancing in a corner from David Beckham before sprinting back to the centre to get the game restarted. Goals from Dwight Yorke and Andy Cole then secured United's place in the Champions League final for the first time in 31 years.

On the jubilant flight back to Manchester, Ferguson confided in United's head of security Ned Kelly: "I never thought I would say this, but he's actually a better player than Bryan Robson."

"No matter how many people tell me I deserve that

Champions League medal, I know I don't," said Keane in his autobiography. "In fact, you could argue my indiscipline came very close to costing us the treble."

In the following season Keane cemented his position as the country's leading player, captaining United to another title and finishing the season by winning the Footballer of the Year award.

I was at the Royal Lancaster Hotel in London to watch him accept his trophy and he looked distinctly uncomfortable, like an awkward teenager, as he gave his acceptance speech.

"Oh Jesus, that was the most nervous I have ever been," he would later tell me. "Everyone was being so nice, and saying lovely things about me that I felt really embarrassed. I just thought, 'Jesus! Get me out of here!' Some people, with more confidence, might have liked it, but it really wasn't my thing."

Keane was always the antidote to football's burgeoning celebrity culture, famously willing to criticise the "prawn sandwich" corporate fans that didn't give the club enough support at Old Trafford. He was the anti-David Beckham. He did not have an agent, and never courted attention. "I'm not comfortable with the adulation," he once told me. "Some might enjoy it, but I don't. I like the respect you get for being a footballer, but the rest is a load of crap. I wouldn't idolise a footballer."

Keane was always a bit different, something of a

loner, for while he engineered a team spirit in his United sides, he also said he wouldn't send his teammates a Christmas card, ask them out for a drink, and didn't have any of their phone numbers. Gary Neville tells a story of texting Keane with his new mobile number, and receiving a text straight back from him, which said: "So what."

While Keane could be blunt, I always enjoyed interviewing him. Even if there was always a sense of trepidation to it as well, for he didn't suffer fools, and would let you know about it, from his vice-like handshake to his intense all-knowing stare. A photographer I worked with once asked Keane to growl in to the camera. "I'm a footballer, not a f***ing actor," he replied.

But Keane could be charming and affable too, far removed from the menacing vein-bulging figure wearing a red shirt. Once he got going he could actually enjoy himself too, on one occasion rather than cut short an interview with me, he instead asked his wife Theresa to pick up their three children from school.

The truth is he was a dream to interview, because he was always brutally honest, he never ducked a question, and simply gave it to you straight.

The last time I interviewed him was in April 2001, the morning after United had lost the first leg of the Champions League quarter-final to Bayern Munich. I feared he might be surly and uncooperative, but the defeat had left him in a reflective mood.

Even though United were on the brink of winning a third consecutive Premier League title, the failure to get back to the Champions League final troubled him. He had things he wanted to get off his chest.

"We have to be careful to think that our success is going to go on and on. We have to start dominating Europe as well as the Premiership. It is up to the manager to know when to move people on," he said.

"I have seen United players getting complacent, thinking they've done it all and getting carried away by a bit of success. All you have to do is drop your standards by 5 per cent or 10 per cent and it's obvious, especially in Europe."

"You can see it in training when players just go through the motions. You can't do that, you always have to give your best. It's up to the manager to spot it, maybe I'll help him."

The interview was the cover story for *FourFourTwo* magazine, but after being published the tabloids all picked it up, and *The Daily Mirror* splashed it across their back page as "The most explosive interview of the year." I was told Ferguson was furious at the headlines and had hauled Keane in to his office.

In the summer of 2002 Keane's refusal to bite his tongue saw him walk out on the Republic of Ireland on the eve of the World Cup finals in Japan. In my interview he had called part of the Irish set-up an "absolutely disgrace," and a year later nothing had changed when he arrived for the tournament.

Keane stewed on the poor training ground in Saipan, the inappropriate food and the fact the training kit was late, and became steadily more angry, before unleashing his fury at what he perceived to be this amateurish approach in two newspaper interviews.

The Ireland manager Mick McCarthy was incensed and called a team meeting in which he accused Keane of faking an injury and not being committed. According to Keane's autobiography, it drew this response from him: "Mick, you're a liar... you're a f***ing wanker. I didn't rate you as a player, I don't rate you as a manager, and I don't rate you as a person. You're a f***ing wanker and you can stick your World Cup up your arse."

Back at United, in the final years of his Old Trafford career, Keane would alter his game, making less surging runs, and instead sitting in the centre of midfield, organising his teammates and expertly distributing the ball.

"The old Roy Keane of charging all over the pitch has gone," said the man himself at the time. "Before I ran around and tried to do everything. Now I am trying to use my head more. "It dawned on me: 'Jesus, Roy, let the others do a bit of running, they're fit lads'. I am going to be a bit cleverer."

It was enough to captain United to another Premier League title in 2003 and the FA Cup in 2004. As his manager observed: "He is a far more measured player now, more of a thinking player. Five years ago, maybe he lived on his raw energy. Now you see a mature player. He is a player at his very peak."

Having recovered from a hip injury, which was thought might have even ended his career, and could require a hip replacement in retirement, Keane took more care of his body, embracing yoga sessions and hot stone massages.

But it was never going to quell the fire inside him. He would be sent off 11 times for United, the first in 1995 and the last in 2004, with the most infamous being when he took his revenge on Alf-Inge Haaland in the Manchester derby at Old Trafford in April 2001.

He had never forgiven the Norwegian for standing over him and accusing him of faking his cruicate injury at Elland Road. In between the two incidents, I asked Keane if he carried a grudge against Haaland? "No, not me," he said, but at the time, I wrote "his smiling eyes say differently."

In his autobiography, Keane writes about the motivation behind his horrific thigh-challenge on Haaland. "I'd waited long enough. I f***ing hit him hard. The ball was there (I think). Take that you c***. And don't ever stand over me sneering about fake injuries." This account would earn him a five-match ban.

It was in his final full season in March 2005 inside the

tight tunnel at Highbury that possibly the defining image of Keane's career occurred. Lining up to face Arsenal, the reigning champions and Invincibles of the previous season, Keane saw his nemesis Patrick Vieira attempting to intimidate Gary Neville.

An outraged Keane shouted, "You, Vieira, come and pick on me." With his eyes blazing, he pointed to the pitch, and added "I'll see you out there." Keane had set the tone for the game: 'Stick behind me lads, we'll sort this' was his message. He played the whole game with a controlled anger and on this occasion didn't even get booked as he inspired United to a 4-2 win over the champions.

Keane's restless anger, once such a vital part of his armour, would eventually lead to his downfall. In the autumn of 2005 he was invited on to MUTV to discuss United's 4-1 defeat at Middlesbrough, even though he hadn't played. It was a strange choice, never destined to end well.

Keane proceeded to do what he always did, and told the brutal truth. Having seen United miss out first to Arsenal and then Chelsea in the last two league campaigns, and seeing little evidence this was about to change in the current season, Keane's pent-up anger at his young teammates boiled over.

The show never made it on to the air, having first been shown to the United Chief Executive David Gill, who decided to ban it, but details inevitably leaked.

Keane had broken with protocol by singling out

individual players. It was reported he said of Rio Ferdinand: "Just because you're paid £120,000 a week...you think you are a superstar"; Darren Fletcher is spoken about with contempt: "I can't understand why people in Scotland rave about Darren Fletcher"; Kieran Richardson is described as "a lazy defender," while Alan Smith's role as a makeshift midfielder prompts the observation: "He doesn't know what he is doing."

It took Ferguson two weeks to reach the reluctant, but inevitable, decision that Keane had gone too far and would have to go.

On the morning of November 18, 2005, Keane was called in to Ferguson's office and told in a brief meeting he was being let go. He had known what was coming and had cleaned out his locker the night before, so he could disappear quickly without any goodbyes, leaving Ferguson to make the announcement to the rest of the squad that their captain had left the team.

He joined Celtic for six months, picking up a Scottish Premier League title and a Scottish League Cup, before moving into management, first winning the Championship title and promotion to the Premier League with Sunderland, before failing to make an impression at Ipswich Town over 21 months.

Six years after leaving Old Trafford, Keane is still revered as the club's greatest ever captain, but for the moment, the feeling doesn't appear mutual. He is still resisting any slump into sentimentality.

"I'm pretty sure [United] have wiped me from their history and I have wiped them from mine, so I have no interest whatsoever," he said back in 2010. "It's pretty scary actually, you move on. You always have a little interest in your old team [and] I'd have that with Rockmount, Cobh, Sunderland, Forest, Celtic. But if you think I'm waiting and hoping [United] win trophies I'm not."

IX. RYAN GIGGS

Left midfield

The Medal Collector

Honours 1991- end of 2011-12 season – 909 appearances (163 goals); Premier League 1993, 1994, 1996, 1997, 1999, 2000, 2001, 2003, 2007, 2008, 2009, 2011; FA Cup 1994, 1996, 1999, 2004; Champions League 1999, 2008; League Cup 1992, 2006, 2009; Inter-Continental Cup 1999; World Club Championship 2008; European Super Cup 1991

In the team because no one has ever played with such sustained brilliance for so long, and won so much. A unique player

Quote "Ryan Giggs has always epitomised what is best about football" – Brian Kidd

Greatest moment Beating almost half the Arsenal side to score *that* dramatic winner in the 1999 FA Cup semi-final replay

DURING THE SUMMER of 2010, Ryan Giggs was clearing out some drawers at home when he found a Champions League winners medal, his OBE and a couple of Premier League title winners' medals hidden in the back of one. "I had no idea they were there, I had forgotten about them," he said.

When you are the most successful footballer in the history of the British game, it can be difficult to account for all your honours, and when I asked, Giggs wasn't even sure how many he had won.

At the end of the 2010-11 season the correct answer was 24 winners medals from major competitions (12 Premier League titles, four FA Cups, three League Cups, two Champions Leagues, one Intercontinental Cup, one FIFA Club World Cup and one European Super Cup), and when you throw in Charity Shields, and runners-up medals too, it expands to a staggering 45.

But you will find none of these medals on display at Giggs' family house on the outskirts of Manchester; no pictures, framed shirts or mementoes either, nothing at all. "If you walked in to my house you wouldn't even know I was a footballer," he said.

While the Chelsea and England captain John Terry built an entire annex to his house to display his medals, including mannequins behind glass dressed in his old shirts, Giggs has never had any interest in creating such a shrine to himself, and instead donates most of his medals to be displayed at the

Old Trafford museum.

"I've never seen the need for it really," he told me. "I have got 50 years to go on about how much I've won. I'm not being blasé – I am proud of what I've achieved, but looking at a medal or talking about what I've won doesn't do anything for me."

For over two decades it is this lack of sentiment, combined with a fierce determination to keep on winning, that has seen Giggs enjoy a career of unprecedented success and become recognised as one of the game's greatest ever players.

A naturally modest character, he has long been the popular face of Manchester United, which saw him, to his visible shock, become only the fifth footballer in over half a century to be voted by the public as the BBC's Sports Personality of the Year in 2009.

Giggs has the same universal appeal as Sir Bobby Charlton, who he overtook as United's all-time appearance maker in 2008, which at the end of 2011 now stands at 889 games and counting. Earlier in 2011 Giggs was voted the greatest player in Manchester United's history in a worldwide poll of the club's fans.

I am the same age as Giggs. He has been playing for so long that when he made his debut I was in sixth form at school. I've watched his whole career unfold and now I attend games with my six year-old son Louis, who has Giggs' number 11 printed on the back of his United shirt.

As United have dominated English football over the last two decades, Giggs – the only player to have played *and* scored in each of the first 20 Premier League seasons – has been the one constant in each of Sir Alex Ferguson's trophy-winning sides.

At first he was the prodigious teenager with the mop of curly hair surrounded by Peter Schmeichel, Steve Bruce and Eric Cantona when United won the first ever Premier League, then the Double in the early '90s.

As his career progressed, he became the leader of Fergie's Fledglings, alongside David Beckham, Paul Scholes and Gary Neville, who emerged to win another double in their first season together, before trumping that with the Treble in 1999.

In his later years, at the end of the '90s, and into another decade, he has served as the club's elder statesman, and at times the club captain, lifting another Champions League in 2008, and four more Premier League titles. The older Giggs has helped to guide the youthful talents of Wayne Rooney, Cristiano Ronaldo and Javier Hernandez while still competing at the highest level.

But what is most remarkable about Giggs is there has never been any discernible dip in form, especially in his later years. As he has got older he has never had to trade on former glories, but rather reinvented the rules for the ageing player and got better.

As a testament to his longevity, he was voted the

PFA Player of the Year in 2009 – at age 35, the oldest player to ever win it – a full seventeen years after he won the first of his two PFA Young Player of the Year awards in 1992.

In this time Giggs evolved from a youthful blur of energy on the left flank, beating defenders with sheer pace, into a wiser and more complete player, just as comfortable in the centre, while managing to keep most of the natural cut and thrust of his younger game.

It is difficult to even pinpoint the peak of his career, for he doesn't seem to have ever reached it. As Sir Alex Ferguson once said, "There's just been no discernible deterioration in his game at all. He is just an incredible human being who defies logic. There is no other player who has done what he's done or is ever likely to. He is quite an amazing man."

Giggs is blessed with an extraordinary combination of pace, balance, close control, athleticism, and an instinctive and clinical finish. Ferguson has long talked about how he floated, not ran, along the wing, swaying and changing direction at speed, giving defenders, "twisted blood."

It all came so naturally to Giggs. After all, it was in his genes. His father, Danny Wilson had been a talented professional rugby league player for Swinton during the '80s, and grainy footage testifies to how he could effortlessly glide and sway over a pitch like his son.

"I know how good he is because I have to play against him in training," said Gary Neville. "Giggsy has just got everything. He is brave, he is elusive, he is quick and he works hard. He has got a different level of stamina to everyone else at the club. If Giggsy decides he wants to go full out, he just breezes past you. It is almost like he is taking the mickey."

"He's got a steely way about him, on and off the pitch," added Neville. "I've hardly ever seen him raise his voice, but he doesn't need to. He's slight, but people know he's not to be messed with."

However, Giggs always strived to play the game the right way. He is rarely booked, incredibly never sent off for United, and never took a dive; Ferguson has even joked he doesn't go down enough.

Giggs boasts a stunning show reel of goals. He scores goals that lift you off your seat, make you realise just why you love football, and linger long in the memory.

There was the nutmeg and acceleration to leave behind a gaggle of Spurs defenders at White Hart Lane in 1992; the nonchalant jinking past most of the QPR defence in 1994; collecting the ball at pace, the dip of the shoulder and the finish into the top corner against Juventus in 1997; and, of course, *that* winner against Arsenal in the 1999 FA Cup semi-final replay, a goal that above all others encapsulates his genius.

It was in December 1986 that Sir Alex Ferguson first

saw a 13 year-old Giggs float across a football pitch. After being tipped off by the United steward Harold Wood about a highly promising player at Deans Sports club who was training at Manchester City wearing his United shirt twice a week, he first sent his scout Joe Brown to watch him before arranging a trial game at the Cliff training ground.

"A gold miner who has searched every part of a river or mountain and then suddenly finds himself staring at a nugget could not feel more exhilaration than I did watching Giggs that day," Ferguson wrote in his autobiography. "My first sight was of him floating over the pitch so effortlessly you would have sworn his feet weren't touching the ground. He carried his head high and looked as relaxed on the park as a dog chasing a piece of silver paper in the wind."

On Giggs' 14th birthday, Ferguson appeared on the doorstep of his mother's house to sign him. "I can honestly say whatever United have paid me... was justified at a stroke by securing Ryan."

Sir Bobby Charlton was entranced the moment he saw Giggs in action, and would specially book days off work to come and watch him play for the youth teams at the Cliff.

Even though he was surrounded by the likes of David Beckham, Paul Scholes, Nicky Butt and Gary Neville, it was Giggs who stood out. There were doubts about whether each of the youngsters would make it, except for Giggs. The evidence was too compelling;

he was bound to be a star.

Ferguson handed Giggs a first team debut at 17 as a substitute against Everton at Old Trafford in March 1991. He made his first start against Manchester City two months later, and scored the winner in a 1-0 victory, though he admits he probably didn't get the last touch.

In his first full season, 1991-92, Giggs made an immediate impact on the left wing, dislodging the reigning PFA Young Player of the Year Lee Sharpe and winning the award himself.

He retained the award in the following season as a part of the United side that became champions for the first time since 1967, providing a constant threat on the left wing and scoring 11 goals. During the summer of 1993, Ferguson turned down a bid of £10 million from AC Milan, then just short of a world record transfer fee.

Young, good-looking and supremely talented, Giggs became the poster boy for the game at the dawn of the Premier League era. He was signed up by a legion of sponsors, wrote his autobiography at only 20, was mobbed wherever he went and once drew up to 10,000 fans to a shop opening in Swansea.

"I first realised how famous I had become in the summer of 1993 when we went on a pre-season tour of South Africa," Giggs once told me. "At a function I was approached by a gentleman who said, 'Excuse me, Nelson Mandela would like to meet you.' I couldn't believe it. My only reaction was to say, 'What? He's heard of me.' So I went over there and had a brief chat with him, totally in awe."

As the old guard of Cantona, Hughes, Sharpe and Kanchelskis all moved on, Giggs would become one of United's main source of inspiration. He helped them step up in the Champions League with memorable goals and performances against Porto and Juventus, and throughout most of the Treble-winning season.

His defining moment came against Arsenal on April 14 1999 in the FA Cup semi-final replay at Villa Park. On as a substitute, Giggs had been listless until the 110th minute of extra-time when he picked up a stray pass from Patrick Vieira and headed towards goal.

"It was all instinct, there was no one in front of me, so I just put my head down and went towards the goal," Giggs told me. "There was no way I was going to pass it. I skipped past a challenge from Vieira, then Dixon and Vieira again. I was then in between Dixon and Keown, and I got past them to give me a shot at David Seaman. My thought was just to hit it as hard as I could."

As the French legend, and former Monaco and Fulham manager Jean Tigana once observed, "He is the detonator, the man who makes United explode," while the England manager Fabio Capello, then still in Italy, would marvel at his "special fantasia."

There would be injuries and disappointments, but most of the time the winners' medals and trophies continued to be added at an impressive rate to be stuffed down the back of a drawer.

The only regret Giggs harbours is never playing at a major championship with Wales. A former England schoolboy captain – who was born in Cardiff before moving to Manchester aged seven – he elected to play for the land of his birth and parents and became the youngest ever Welsh international at 17 years and 321 days in 1991. He would win a total of 64 caps, but his commitment to international football was doubted as for many years he didn't play in a single friendly, before retiring in 2007.

When Giggs entered his thirties, and the flecks of grey started to appear on his temples, he made the conscious decision not to slow down, but instead he wanted to get better.

"Footballers will tell you your life changes after 30, it is the beginning of the end. I was determined that wouldn't happen to me. I didn't want to be judged like that, and since I got into my 30s I have been at my happiest, and have played some of my best football, because as I have got older I make less rash decisions."

The secret of Giggs' success has largely been due to twice-weekly yoga sessions, regular trips to the osteopath and acupuncturist to ward off injuries, and a strict diet, which involves almost no alcohol, and avoiding even having butter on his toast, which makes him feel sluggish. This produced, "a new man", according to Ferguson.

In the new millennium, with Rooney and Ronaldo the new stars of Old Trafford, Giggs held his own, scoring the decisive goal against Wigan to secure the 2008 Premier League title before scoring the winning penalty against Chelsea in the shoot-out in Moscow to win the Champions League.

"The purest serendipity" is how Giggs described winning the title on the day he equalled Sir Bobby Charlton's all-time appearance record in his 758th game, and then overtaking it in the very next match against Chelsea in Moscow. He has had that sort of career.

Amid the celebrations back at their hotel in the early hours of the morning after winning the Champions League, Charlton himself presented Giggs with a watch inscribed with the new record '759', as his teammates sang his terrace anthems, 'Giggs will tear you apart again' and 'Ryan Giggs running down the wing'.

A year later he would overshadow his younger teammates again by beating them to the PFA Player of the Year award in 2009. Since then two more Premier League titles have been added, and in November 2011 when Giggs turned 38 – the same age as George Best found himself spending Christmas in Pentonville Prison – he remained an influential and leading member of the United side.

Inside the Old Trafford dressing room, Giggs is revered by the younger players, who he hands out advice and discipline to in equal measure. "He is like a God [to them]," says Ferguson, while his teammate John O'Shea has observed, "He knows when to bring people down a peg or two with a quiet word."

I first got to know Giggs in the late '90s, and have met and interviewed him several times since, including a period when I helped launch his website, which involved speaking to him a couple of times a week during the season to update his diary.

I wouldn't profess to know him intimately, I once asked if an interviewer ever saw the real him? "No, probably not," he said.

But over the years it struck me he never seemed to change. He always lacked the narcissism of so many modern players.

The last time I saw him in the autumn of 2010, he arrived at our photo shoot for *Sky Sports Magazine* without the usual baggage of fame. There was no agent, no publicist, no entourage at all; just him, arriving without any fuss.

He was always warm and engaging company, candid and open, unfailingly polite, and regularly displayed the dry sense of humour not always obvious in his more guarded on camera personality.

In his early years he actively cultivated a bland

image; it made it easier for him to deal with life in the spotlight. But in the dressing room his teammates knew a different side. "He's a Salford lad, streetwise and wickedly funny," said Roy Keane in his autobiography. "Innocent Giggsy is not. He's got away with murder over the years, and he laughs about it."

In his later years he became a very good and valued talker about the game, so it is a shame he has inevitably retreated since his private life became tabloid fodder for several months early in 2011.

It was thought this uncomfortable time could tarnish his legacy, but his achievements in football are too great and too unique to do that.

"Busby, Ferguson, Charlton and Giggs, that's the quartet who sit at the top of this club," Gary Neville once said. "You can separate them from everyone else with their longevity, games, and medals, and also the way they embody everything that's great about United."

In that last meeting, I asked Giggs how he looked back at the previous two decades.

"I suppose I have fulfilled my potential," he laughed. "I wouldn't swap my career for anyone in football's, I have won so much and been a part of so many great teams, and played next to so many wonderful players. I have been very lucky."

X. DENIS LAW

Centre forward

The King

Honours 1962-1973 – 404 appearances (237 goals); First Division Championship 1965, 1967; FA Cup 1963

In the team because no one thrilled the Stretford End and scored as many goals as Denis Law

Quote "If you had to send somebody out to score a goal to save your life, there could be only one man: the Lawman" – Manchester United assistant manager Jimmy Murphy

Greatest moment Lifting his first League Championship at the end of the 1964-65 season as United's leading scorer with 39 goals.

DENIS LAW HAS a confession: "I never wanted to be a goal scorer."

"I was always reluctant playing that role," he told me in the autumn of 2011. "I started out as an inside-forward, and preferred that because I could get up and down the pitch, and be involved in the whole game. But at United, Sir Matt told me not to come back in to our own half, just to stay up front and score the goals."

Law did a fine job hiding his annoyance and duly followed Sir Matt Busby's instructions to become the most prolific and natural striker in the history of Manchester United.

It came as a surprise Law didn't completely enjoy being a goal scorer, for he was born to do it, possessing a rare ability to get on the end of chances and guide the ball into the back of the net.

"If you had to send somebody out to score a goal to save your life, there could be only one man, the Lawman," eulogised the Manchester United assistant manager Jimmy Murphy.

"Once we had got Denis to Old Trafford he turned into the most exciting player in the game," Sir Matt Busby once said. "He was the quickest thinking player I ever saw, quicker than anyone. He had tremendous acceleration and could leap to enormous heights to head the ball with unbelievable accuracy."

"He has the courage to take on the biggest and most ferocious opponents, and when a chance was on for him, even only a half-chance, whether he had his back to goal, or was side on, or the ball was on the deck or up by shoulder height, he would have it in the net with such power and acrobatic agility you could only gasp."

At Manchester United Law scored 237 goals in 404 games – second only to his teammate Sir Bobby Charlton in the all-time scoring list – and he set club records for the most goals in the FA Cup (34, which still stands) and in Europe, with 28 goals in 33 games.

There are only three statues at Old Trafford and Law features in two of them. At the front of the East Stand, he stands on a grand plinth alongside George Best and Bobby Charlton, opposite one of Sir Matt Busby casting his eye across the forecourt.

Inside the stadium Law is the subject of the only statue of an individual player. On the concourse of the upper tier of the Stretford End – where Law's most passionate fans once stood – he is immortalised as a towering 12-foot bronze figure, wheeling away with a typically impish grin and one arm in the air to celebrate yet another goal.

Law was the 'King of the Stretford End' long before Eric Cantona was crowned by a later generation, although he told me the title "was embarrassing, because it made me look like a big head."

The Stretford End worshipped the Scotsman for all he gave to them, and as Sir Matt Busby noted, he became one of the first British players to make a point of saluting the crowd after each of his goals.

Law was the player working class Manchester lads packed onto the Stretford End every other Saturday afternoon most wanted to be, the one they could most relate to. While Best was too cool and Charlton too straight, Law was the cheeky and abrasive lad, forever grateful to be on the pitch and giving absolutely everything.

There was a constant energy about him; Charlton talks about his electricity and how sparks would fly off him, because he did everything at speed; forever seeking a chance, bobbing and weaving, anticipating, harassing opponents, losing his marker, and when a chance arrived he would ruthlessly dispatch it.

"I picked up the scraps, the six-yard box was my area, anything farther than the penalty spot was too far for me," he has said.

On pitches Law would dismiss as "mud heaps", and in an era when strikers had little protection and defenders were often allowed to cut them down at will, he had little fear, throwing his relatively slight frame into tackles if he thought it could lead to a goal.

As his Manchester City teammate from the early '60s Ken Barnes once said, "He was a skinny little bugger, but he had a bit of the devil about him, no one took liberties with him."

The son of a fisherman, and the youngest of seven children, Law grew up in what he recalls as relative poverty in the bleak years following the Second World War, sleeping three to a bed, wearing hand-me down clothes and believing orange juice was a luxury.

Law honed his famous aggression on the playgrounds of Aberdeen, playing football with just one eye open as he had a squint and refusing to be cowed by the bullies who called him "cock-eyed."

At 15 he was invited down to Huddersfield, and greeted by a sceptical Bill Shankly, who once said, "He looked like a skinned rabbit, my first reaction was to get him on the first train home."

But Shankly fed him a diet of steak and milk and soon came to appreciate him, as did Sir Matt Busby. After watching him play for Huddersfield against United in an FA Cup Youth tie in September 1956, Busby swiftly offered £10,000, an unprecedented amount for a 16 year-old yet to make his first team debut.

Huddersfield refused to budge, and Busby would have to wait another six years to bring his man to Old Trafford. Law first joined Manchester City for a British record fee of £55,000 in March 1960 before moving on after just more than a year to spend a largely unhappy season in Italy with Torino.

"I adored the food, clothes, and lifestyle, but I found playing the actual game a joyless experience," he told me. "I went there too young, and the truth is it was simply for the money."

In the summer of 1962 Law had the opportunity to stay in Italy with Juventus, but was relieved to return to Manchester when United signed him for another British record fee of £115,000. "I've got you at last son," Busby gleefully told him.

In the previous four years United had simply got by, still ravaged by the loss of so many players at Munich, but the signing of Law was a catalyst and galvanised the club once again.

"Denis provided that vital spark that could make all the difference, there was always a touch of stardust about him, as my wife said, 'The game always seemed more exciting when Denis played'," said the United defender Bill Foulkes.

"He hit Old Trafford like a flash of lightning, breathing new life into the team with his fearlessness, his self-belief and his astonishing ability to score goals out of nothing," recalled Charlton. "Now United were radiating confidence again and so much of that was done to Denis."

Law's impact was immediate, he scored seven minutes in to his United debut, and finished as the side's leading scorer with 29 goals, which included one against Leicester City in the FA Cup final at Wembley to help deliver United their first trophy since Munich.

The goals kept coming, a total of 46 in the following season – which saw him become the first Scottish player to be voted European Footballer of the Year – while another 39 in the 1964-65 season helped United return to the summit as League Champions.

As the 'Holy Trinity' of Best, Law and Charlton ran amok – "It was a truly amazing time," says Law – another League title followed in 1967, with Law contributing 25 goals. But sadly for him, when the defining moment of this era arrived he was absent.

On the night of May 28, 1968, he was not alongside his teammates on the pitch at Wembley, or even in the stands. He was sitting in a hospital bed in Manchester recovering from major surgery to his knee and watching on television as United won the European Cup with a 4-1 victory over Benfica.

"I watched with a can of McEwans and a group of nuns," Law told me. "It was hard to miss that night, and I have never enjoyed watching football on television. I consoled myself with the thought we would get back to the final again, but we never did."

By the early '70s injuries would begin to take a heavy toll on Law. The mind was still sharp but the lightning reflexes had been dulled and the goals no longer came so easily.

"I was never the same player after my knee injury," Law admitted. "I had surgery, but it was more like butchery of the highest standard. Looking back, I would have asked more questions about it. This was my life and livelihood but after the surgery I played in constant pain and lost much of my game."

At the end of the 1972-73 season an ailing Law suffered the undeserved indignity of learning from a television report that he had been allowed to leave Old Trafford on a free transfer.

That summer he crossed town to rejoin Manchester City and at the end of that season fate cruelly dictated Law would return to Old Trafford with Tommy Docherty's side on the brink of relegation.

The events of April 27, 1974 are painfully seared into Law's memory. With nine minutes remaining, Francis Lee crossed the ball into the penalty area for Law to almost apologetically back heel it past Alex Stepney to win the game for City.

It is known as the goal that relegated United, but that is not true. As Law is keen to remind anyone, United were down anyway, they could have beaten City 10-0 that afternoon and it would have made no difference. But the myth is sustained by it's powerful symbolism; the returning hero consumed with remorse at condemning his beloved side to the Second Division.

It might have been the winning goal in a derby game but for Law it remains, "the most painful memory of my career... it was the first time I'd ever scored a goal that made me feel sad."

Enquiries about the goal now are often met simply with "Next question" and a knowing look. A normally jovial character, Law isn't being rude, it just remains too painful to talk about. When I broached the subject myself, he would only say: "I don't think about it, honestly I don't. I certainly don't like talking about it."

Law would play on for a couple of months; his final game was for Scotland against Zaire at the 1974 World Cup in West Germany, before retiring in August that year. "It took me a long time to adjust to life. When you're used to playing in front of 60,000 each week you're up in the clouds, and then you have to come back to reality."

A proud Scot, he told me the highlight of his career came not at Old Trafford, but each time he wore the dark blue of Scotland. "That was sheer paradise... nothing came close to running out in front of 130,000 people at Hampden Park." He remains Scotland's joint all-time goalscorer with 30 goals from 55 games (Kenny Dalglish needed another 47 games to score the same amount) and in 2000 was voted Scotland's greatest ever player by *The Daily Record*.

When the Celtic legend Danny McGrain was new to the Scotland squad in 1973 he recalls being petrified about meeting such an icon of the world game. "I half expected Denis would walk through the door surrounded by white mist, like some celestial being."

While Sir Alex Ferguson is a contemporary of Law's –

they were born only 22 months apart – the striker has always been the United manager's hero.

"Anyone who has the slightest doubt about Denis' stature in the game might care to heed the words of no less eminent a judge than Pele," Ferguson has said. "He once said the only British player who could get into the Brazil team was Denis Law. I rest my case."

These days Law still lives on the outskirts of Manchester, but rarely ventures back to Old Trafford, or even the Etihad Stadium, to watch either of his old teams. He says, simply, "I don't really enjoy watching football these days, even at home on the television."

But on the rare occasions he does venture down Sir Matt Busby Way to the old stadium he graced for eleven years he makes sure he glances up at that statue of himself, Bobby Charlton and George Best. "I do feel quite proud to see us all standing there together."

XI. ERIC CANTONA

Centre forward
The Catalyst

Honours 1992-1997 – 185 appearances (82 goals);
Premier League 1993, 1994, 1996, 1997; FA Cup
1994, 1996

In the team because his charisma and genius
defined United for nearly five years, and delivered
unprecedented success

Quote "Eric was the catalyst for the championships.
He brought a vision we did not have before... He was
a phenomenal player" – Sir Alex Ferguson

Greatest moment Returning from his eight-month
ban to lead a young United side to the League and FA
Cup double in 1996

THE CALL CAME through on an ordinary Tuesday morning. "Can you interview Eric Cantona tomorrow?" The magazine editor who was asking already knew the answer, for this wasn't work. He was more doing me a favour and offering the chance to meet a hero.

My first thought was to locate my camera and marker pen, rather than my tape recorder. A decade after he retired, Cantona still unashamedly brought out the fan in me rather than the detached journalist.

I had joined *Manchester United magazine* in the summer of 1996, but didn't get the opportunity to speak to Cantona before he retired nine months later. The truth is he didn't speak to the English press then – not even to the club's official magazine or programme.

Now in the spring of 2006, Cantona was being more talkative on behalf of his sponsors Nike in the suite of a London hotel.

It was only a short interview, in which I asked him choose his own Best XI from his favourite players, which included Diego Maradona, George Best, Garrincha, Mario Kempes, Johan Cruyff, and just one of his former United teammates, Roy Keane.

 I have interviewed many famous sports people before without being remotely star struck but this was different. This was Eric.

I'm glad I took my tape-recorder as I didn't do much

listening in my twenty minutes with him, being too preoccupied with thinking, 'That's Eric sitting opposite me, I'm talking to Eric Cantona' and when the interview was over I asked to have a picture with him.

Eric had this sort of effect on United fans of my generation. He was probably my last genuine United hero, when footballers were still older than me and you could look up to them.

In the film *Looking for Eric*, he says, "I am not a man, I am Cantona." It is a brilliant line, delivered with a knowing smile, because he was always more than just another footballer.

United fans came to believe he personified the club with his swagger, his attitude, his rebellious spirit, his effortless style and his ability to seemingly do whatever he wanted.

He inspired a blind devotion that hasn't been seen since and has only ever been matched by probably Denis Law and George Best. His name is still lustily sung at Old Trafford today.

In 2001, Cantona was voted by United fans as the club's greatest player of all-time, ahead of George Best and Ryan Giggs.

His character has always been overanalysed; his initial appeal was simply that he was a bit different, at a time when he was one of only 11 foreigners at the inception of the Premier League.

He didn't conform to the usual stereotype, appearing to be more artistic and cerebral than most footballers. He liked to paint and had an interest in literature and philosophy.

But he also enjoyed this mystique. Seeming distant and inscrutable, it was no surprise he would later act, for he played a role. His teammates all say he spoke good English but pretended otherwise.

"Cast as the brooding, temperamental prima donna, Eric was in reality one of the lads, that was his game, especially with the media," Roy Keane has observed. "The eccentric loner was his public mask, part of what he wanted, professionally, to be."

He rarely gave interviews and much of his public image was skillfully shaped in a series of Nike adverts, so any public utterances he made – on seagulls and trawlers, for instance – were examined in great detail. But as he admitted, "I talk a lot of bullshit."

Most importantly, Cantona was revered for helping deliver a period of success Manchester United had never known before.

It is difficult to fully appreciate just how different United were when Cantona arrived in November 1992. Alex Ferguson had been there for six years and built a decent cup side but burdened by history, they had not won the league for a quarter of a century.

United had come close the previous season but like

so often before, collapsed within sight of the trophy. The banner held aloft at Anfield that read, 'Have you ever seen United win the League?' hurt because it was true. Most United fans had never seen it.

Four and a half years later, when Cantona suddenly left Old Trafford, he had helped United win four Premier League titles, as well as adding two FA Cups as part of two Doubles in 1994 and 1996.

In 185 games for United, Cantona scored 82 goals and provided an incredible 66 assists. When he was on the team sheet United won 66 per cent of games, drew 23 per cent and lost only 11 per cent.

"Eric was the catalyst for the championships," Sir Alex Ferguson has said. "He brought a vision we did not have before. We were getting there but he certainly accelerated it. He was a phenomenal player."

"Of all the many qualities a good team must possess, the supreme essential for me is penetration, and Eric brought the can-opener."

At 26 Cantona joined United as something of a footballing nomad, having passed through seven clubs in his career so far.

Born in Marseille, Cantona started under Guy Roux at Auxerre, but after a loan spell at Martigues, he joined Marseille where he won a French title with them in 1989. However he never properly settled and was sent out on loan first to Bordeaux, and then

Montpellier, where he won the French Cup in 1990.

On his return Cantona helped Marseille win the French title again in 1991 but that summer he was on the move again to Nimes.

A restless character, never finding the love and trust he craved, he possessed a famously explosive temper, prompting one French official to observe, "behind you is a trail of the smell of sulphur."

In September 1988, he was indefinitely banned from international football for calling the France manger Henri Michel "the most incompetent manager in the world" and "a shit bag."

He also threw his shirt at a referee at Marseille, his boots into a teammate's face at Montpellier, and when he was penalised for a foul for Nimes against St Etienne, he threw the ball at the referee. That incident, in December 1991, earned Cantona a four-game ban but rather than show remorse he called each member of the disciplinary committee an "idiot". They responded by extending his ban to two months, prompting him to announce his retirement from football at the age of 25.

On the recommendation of the French manager Michel Platini, and his assistant Gerard Houllier, he fled to England in January 1992. After a trial at Sheffield Wednesday and with Ferguson already showing interest, the Leeds manager Howard Wilkinson acted quickest and brought him to Elland Road from Nimes for £1million.

Wilkinson would call it, "the biggest gamble of my career," as he had never seen him play in the flesh. But it appeared to pay off as Cantona, often used as a substitute, played in 15 games and contributed three goals to help Leeds hold off United to win the 1992 First Division title.

Cantona would start the new season with a hat-trick in a 4-3 win over Liverpool in the Charity Shield but Wilkinson never fully understood or trusted him. He kept him out of the team and would ultimately drop him as Leeds' title defence imploded that season.

Wilkinson once branded Cantona "unmanageable" and after they had parted would add, "Eric likes to do what he likes, when he likes, because he likes it, and then f*** off. We'd all want a bit of that."

On November 26, 1992, Alex Ferguson was at Old Trafford with his chairman Martin Edwards discussing strikers they might bring to the club after their own poor start to the season and the broken leg suffered by Dion Dublin. They had been knocked out of two cups and had only won one of their previous eight league games.

During their discussion, a call was put through from the Leeds chairman Bill Fotherby enquiring about Denis Irwin. United would not consider selling the Irishman, but while they talked, Ferguson scribbled down a note for Edwards: "Ask him about Cantona". It was soon discovered Leeds were willing to sell and within 24 hours Cantona was being paraded at Old

Trafford.

The story of Cantona's signing has become a cherished anecdote as though he was signed purely by chance in an impulsive moment by Ferguson. But the United manager had long coveted the Frenchman and only weeks before had been alerted by Gerard Houllier to Cantona's unhappiness at Leeds, and likely availability.

United signed Cantona for just £1million, an amount that when Ferguson relayed it to his assistant Brian Kidd, he replied, "For that money, has he lost a leg or something?"

For much of the last decade, Old Trafford had become a striker's graveyard, claiming the reputations of Alan Brazil, Peter Davenport, Garry Birtles and Terry Gibson but Cantona's talent, and his inherent belief in himself, would not allow him to join them.

When Ferguson was giving Cantona a tour of his new home, they reached the centre of the pitch and he turned to the Frenchman and asked, "I wonder if you're good enough to play in this ground?" Cantona replied, "I wonder if Manchester is good enough for me."

It would soon turn into what Cantona called "the perfect marriage," while an equally effusive Ferguson called their union, "the perfect player, at the perfect club at the perfect moment."

After making his debut as a substitute against Manchester City, on only his second start Cantona scored his first United goal against Chelsea at Stamford Bridge. And so begun a run of scoring in four consecutive games to lift United to the top of the Premier League for the first time that season.

United would be there at the end of the season as well to become champions of England for the first time in 26 years.

In that first season, despite arriving just before the halfway point, Cantona scored a total of nine goals in 23 games (the best ratio in the side), contributed the most assists (13) and played a role in half of United's goals. With Eric in the side, United only lost once.

"If ever there was a player in the world who was made for Manchester United, it was Cantona," Ferguson said. "He had been searching all his life for somewhere to call home. Because he had travelled so much, there's a wee bit of a Gypsy about some people, but when he came here he knew this was his place."

At last Cantona had found the trust from a manager he always wanted. Recognising a rare talent, Ferguson undoubtedly indulged his striker, nurturing him, sharing regular cups of tea and attending to his needs. He gave him greater freedom than the other players, whether in training or with the dress code for club functions, causing some teammates to grumble at the double standards, but most accepted it because he helped them win.

Gary Pallister described Cantona's arrival as like a brilliant Formula One team finally finding the right driver. "He made all the difference... he gave us an extra 5 per cent," Peter Schmeichel said.

Cantona had a rare ability to bring the best out of others, whether it was delivering the ball at just the right pace to Ryan Giggs and Andrei Kanchelskis on the flanks, pulling defenders around to allow Paul Ince or Brian McClair the space to surge into, or hovering behind and swapping passes with Mark Hughes up front.

"He was perhaps the best I've played with," Paul Ince once observed. "He seemed to know where anyone was on the pitch at any given time when he had the ball. He used to say to me, 'Treat the ball like you treat a woman, and caress it.' He just loved the ball, didn't he? His little touches, flicks... he was unbelievable."

Lee Sharpe said how, "Cantona had that gift of dragging space around, of having time on the ball, and the vision to find openings and angles which no other player would have seen", while Ryan Giggs appreciated Cantona's ability to always find him and how he took as much pride in creating chances for others as scoring goals.

In the 17 league games United played in the 1992-93 season before Cantona's arrival they scored just 18 goals; in the next 25 games with Cantona they scored 49.

The Frenchman was a blend of a classic number 10 – the playmaker operating between midfield and attack – and a number nine who could play up front on his own and score goals. It is why his biographer Philippe Auclair referred to him as a "nine and a half" style player.

 His teammates could grow frustrated at his lack of tracking back. "Sometimes I'd think, 'F*** it, Eric, you lazy bastard' and then before, or even after, the words were out of my mouth he'd weave a magic spell to score or set up a goal," said Roy Keane.

After enjoying his first proper pre-season at United, Cantona became an even better player, as Ferguson came to describe him as "the fulcrum" of what many regard as United's greatest ever side.

He would score a total of 25 goals that season, his largest total for a campaign at United, as well as setting up another 15.

He scored goals with power, like the 25-yard free-kick against Arsenal at Old Trafford, and with grace and beauty, such as the cushioned touch and looping volley against Wimbledon in the FA Cup.

Cantona had once warned his game came with "dark shadows [and] black stains" but since arriving in England he had largely controlled them until the spring of 1994 when he was sent off twice in three days, firstly with a straight red for an ugly, inexcusable stamp on Swindon Town's John Moncur and then, possibly harshly, for two yellow cards against Arsenal at Highbury.

Despite the ensuing ban, Cantona became the first foreigner to be voted the PFA's Player of the Year, before returning to steady United's title defence, which they would then go on to comfortably retain with an eight point margin over runners-up Blackburn Rovers.

United completed their first ever Double on a wet day at Wembley with a 4-0 win over Chelsea in the FA Cup final. The London side had actually beaten United twice in the league that season and the game had been tight for the first hour until the coolness of Cantona prevailed twice from the penalty spot to settle the game.

The United captain Steve Bruce had told Cantona of his premonition they would win a penalty in the final and recalls, "Eric shrugged his shoulders, threw his arms out and said 'No problem. I'll score."

The following season Cantona's brilliance continued to underpin United's dominance. He scored one and set up another three in a 5-0 win over Manchester City and, in January, he scored a dramatic late winner against Blackburn Rovers to cut their lead at the top of the table.

On the evening of January 25, 1995, United faced Crystal Palace in a testy and ugly game at Selhurst

Park. The Palace captain, and scorer that night, Gareth Southgate, told me his side were proud of their ability to get stuck in and rile opponents, which is what they did that night.

Richard Shaw certainly stuck close to Cantona until in the second half when the Frenchman aimed a kick at him, and for the fifth time in his United career, was sent off.

On his walk back to the tunnel, Cantona's attention was caught by the contorted features of a Palace fan called Matthew Simmons, who had run down eleven rows of the Main Stand to shout what was reported as, "F*** off, you motherf***ing French bastard."

Cantona couldn't ignore the provocation and launched over the advertising hoarding at Simmons with a kick to the chest, followed by a punch to the face, before he was hauled away to the dressing room.

I watched all this unfold from the Arthur Wait stand opposite and would speculate on the drive home that United had now forfeited the league (I was right) because Cantona was bound to be given a 10-match ban (I was wrong; it was to be much, much worse than that.)

Hysteria ensued. Cantona was vilified in the media, with some calling on him to be banned for life. Brian Clough said he should be castrated. I remember thinking at the time how the media had misjudged the mood; it was of course unacceptable – Cantona should serve a long ban – but he should also not have to tolerate such foul and racially motivated abuse from a man it transpired who already had a conviction for assault with intent to rob.

Ferguson had not seen Cantona's kick at Selhurst Park but when he viewed it on television back at home, his first thought was that Eric would have to leave Old Trafford, but soon his protective side prevailed and he refused to bow to those that sought to crucify him.

United took the unilateral decision to fine him two weeks wages and ban him for the rest of the 1994-95 season. But this wasn't enough for the FA, who fined him another £10,000 and extended his ban to October; also stipulating he could not train or play in any practice games. Ferguson said no other player would get that sentence unless they killed the FA chairman Bert Millichip's dog.

He was also charged with assault, and initially jailed for two weeks at Croydon Magistrates Court, but on appeal it was reduced to 120 days community service, which he spent coaching children.

The ban only served to nurture Cantona's legend at United. In his martyrdom he became even more adored, with fans rallying around one of their own in a time of crisis. My wife Esther, then my girlfriend, even wore an 'Eric is Innocent' T-shirt, though clearly he wasn't.

Cantona vowed to come back a changed man, calmer

and more controlled, but also fuelled with a fierce desire to repay those who had not cast him out and remained loyal. "Before that night, I was behaving like a child," he has since said. "I was prepared to repeat the same mistake but I realised it was an irresponsible habit."

On his return Cantona kicked the habit, rather than his opponents. In his first game back on the day his ban expired, October 1, 1995, Liverpool were the visitors to Old Trafford and with his undiminished sense of theatre, Cantona did not disappoint. Setting up United's opening goal for Nicky Butt after five minutes, he also stepped up to score the equalising penalty to earn a 2-2 draw.

During Cantona's ban, Ferguson had moved out some of the old guard, including Paul Ince, Mark Hughes and Andrei Kanchelskis and replaced them with a band of promising youngsters, including Gary Neville, Nicky Butt, David Beckham and Paul Scholes.

Cantona thrived in his new role as a teacher and mentor. "Eric became the player the rest of us wanted to be," David Beckham said. "Watching him in training each day was a football education... I would [also] watch him in the dressing room, checking what he was doing, trying to work out exactly how he prepared for a game."

Cantona was the focus of every game now, as both the defiant United hero, and the cartoon villain, remorselessly booed at every away game. But rather than affect him, it inspired him. He had doused his internal fires and was never sent off again for United.

Roy Keane said he came back "as good as ever," but Peter Schemichel believed he was now "an even better player," who once again was the difference and took charge of United.

In fourteen games during the 1995-96 season, Cantona's goals directly decided games with either a win or a draw for United.

In the spring of 1996, Cantona scored in six successive games, including the winner in 1-0 wins against Arsenal, Tottenham, Coventry, and what would prove to be the title-decider against Newcastle at St James Park, which he celebrated with a cathartic and crazed roar to the heavens.

In the previous season United had stumbled without Cantona, finishing as runners-up to Blackburn but now they regained their title with Cantona, scorer of 19 goals in 38 games in all competitions.

A week later United completed their second Double in three seasons with Cantona scoring the winning goal in the 86th minute of the FA Cup Final against Liverpool, brilliantly readjusting his body on the edge of the penalty box before striking a volley through a crowd of players. He became the first foreign captain to lift the FA Cup.

"The season had been a personal triumph for Eric,"

said Ryan Giggs and in the final symbol of his redemption, Cantona was also voted the Footballer of the Year by many of the same football writers who had roundly condemned him the year before.

The following season would be Cantona's final one at United, though no one had any inkling of this in August, as it began with him lifting the Charity Shield at Wembley after scoring in a 4-0 win over Newcastle United.

But, on reflection, there were signs Cantona was starting to slacken off and lose interest. He began carrying more weight, noticeably on his face and waist and appeared less nimble.

Ryan Giggs has revealed during that season, Cantona had said with "evident self-disgust" that "I didn't know I could play so badly."

It was all relative, as this was Cantona after all. He still scored 15 goals, including arguably his best ever – the run from the halfway line and chip against Sunderland – and was voted United's Player of the Year, while captaining the side to yet another Premier League title.

 On the afternoon Cantona lifted the Premier League trophy at Old Trafford after the final game of the season, he appeared subdued, less willing to celebrate. As Ferguson wrote in his diary, he watched his captain "deep in contemplation" and feared the worse.

Three weeks earlier Cantona had come to Ferguson the morning after Borussia Dortmund had knocked United out of the Champions League semi-final and told him he wanted to retire.

The defeat had greatly affected Cantona. He had been determined to win this competition, to prove something to himself and to those who sneered he too often struggled on the European stage.

It remains the one criticism most levelled at Cantona. In his typically blunt manner Roy Keane has said: "Eric will never rank alongside the truly great European players", while Sir Bobby Charlton has said his failure to assert himself in international and European football has cast a "shadow" over some of this reputation.

While it is true Cantona failed to repeat his Premier League brilliance in Europe, the length of this shadow can be exaggerated.

He has the excellent record of 20 goals in 45 games for France – "I scored one goal in every two games, that's not bad" – and he never enjoyed a proper run in the Champions League. Sent off against Galatasaray in 1993-94, he missed four out of six games for the subsequent ban in 1994-95, before that final season when United reached the semi-finals. However his overall record of five goals in 16 Champions League games is undoubtedly below par for the Frenchman.

At the end of the 1996-97 season, Cantona

confirmed to Ferguson he had played his final game, a week before his 31st birthday. He had his frustrations about how United were using his image in their merchandising – "I gave up, I don't want to be treated like a pair of socks" – and the lack of world-class players coming to United. He also had a strong desire to pursue passions outside of football but ultimately he felt his work was done.

"I didn't want to play any more. I'd lost the passion, I think I retired so young because I wanted to improve every time... [and] I didn't feel that I could improve any more," Cantona has since said.

Cantona disappeared without saying goodbye. His retirement was announced at a press conference by Martin Edwards, prompting a spontaneous wake on the Old Trafford forecourt of distraught and bereft fans. For them, the King was dead.

Nearly a decade and a half after his retirement, Cantona's legacy endures, and in 2008 a worldwide poll held by the Premier League's sponsors Barclays found he remained the most popular player in the history of the competition.

"I do not want any inscription on my tombstone, a blank stone, because I would like to leave behind me the sentiment of a great mystery," Cantona once declared.

A generation of United fans know what should be chiselled on that tombstone: 'The man who made Manchester United great again'.

ABOUT THE AUTHOR

SAM PILGER BEGAN his career as a staff writer, and then deputy editor, on Manchester United magazine in the mid-1990s, regularly interviewing Sir Alex Ferguson, Roy Keane and David Beckham and covering them at the 1999 Champions League final and the inaugural World Club Championships in Brazil. He has also ghosted columns for George Best, Ryan Giggs and Jaap Stam.

In 2000 he moved to FourFourTwo as deputy editor, before going freelance in 2001 to cover a range of sports for publications including The Times Magazine, Esquire, FourFourTwo, Sky Sports Magazine, Inside Cricket and The Cricketer. He has written books, including For Club and Country with Gary and Phil Neville, Manchester United: The Insider Guide, The Treasures of Manchester United, The Ashes Match of My Life, Victory The Battle for the Ashes 2005, and edited The Official Sachin Tendulkar Opus.

A lifelong United fan, who is unlikely to ever surpass his personal record of going to 51 United games in a single season, he now attends games at Old Trafford with his seven year-old son, Louis.

OTHER BEST XI PUBLICATIONS

Best XI Arsenal

Damian Hall, Kevin Whitcher,

Luke Nicoli & Andrew Mangan

Best XI Liverpool

Chris Bascombe, Nick Judd, Ben Lyttleton,

Leo Moynihan & Paul Tomkins

My Best XI Manchester Unitedl

Have a go. Not so easy..

1.

2.

3.

4.

5.

6.

7.

8.

9.

10.

11.

Contact:
bestxi.co.uk
@bestxi
@calmpub

3081829R00081

Printed in Great Britain
by Amazon.co.uk, Ltd.,
Marston Gate.